Vastarien
A LITERARY JOURNAL

Volume Five, Issue One

Jon Padgett, Editor-in-Chief

New Orleans, Louisiana

© 2022 Grimscribe Press

Cover art by Jason Barnett

Interior art by Anna Trueman

Cover design by Anna Trueman

All rights reserved. No part of this publication may be reproduced, distributed, or transmitted in any form or by any means, including photocopying, recording, or other electronic or mechanical methods, without the prior written permission of the publisher, except in the case of brief quotations embodied in critical reviews and certain other noncommercial uses permitted by copyright law.

Published by
Grimscribe Press
New Orleans, LA
USA

grimscribepress.com

CONTENTS

Acknowledgments i

Vastarien Column: Tenebrous Ramblings 1
Romana Lockwood

Halogen Sky 5
Wendy N. Wagner

Twenty-Nine Palms in Reverse 17
Daniel Braum

The Devil's Just Sitting There 31
Laughing: The Uncanny American
Landscapes of Terrence Malick's
Badlands and *Days of Heaven*
Gwendolyn Kiste

Return to Office 41
Kristin Cleaveland

The Case Against the Dream 51
Armel Dagorn

Psithurism 65
T. M. Morgan

For the Night is Long, and I am Lost 77
Without You
Erica Ruppert

"Autopsy on a Puppet": The Day of Lost 87
Illusion in Thomas Ligotti's "Mad Night of
Atonement"
Chris Brawley

Deep Sea Creature 109
Vivian Kasley

Leviathan 115
Lucy Frost

Town Called Malice 117
Lindz McLeod

Coded Dreams: Gender and Information Processing in *The Great God Pan*   125
Macy Harrison

Waiting for Golem   141
Alvaro Zinos-Amaro

Straw World   159
Erik McHatton

The Under Carnival   171
Logan Noble

Fugue   181
Joe Koch

The Flower Imposes Itself on the Ghost House   185
Kolbeinn Karlsson

This Attraction Now Open Till Late   191
Kyla Lee Ward

Itch in the Party House   207
Ivy Grimes

Contributors   217

ACKNOWLEDGMENTS

Thanks to all our benefactors, particularly Robert Ankney, James Michael Baker, Chris Cangiano, Lambrineas D. Epameinondas, Darren Fisher, Richard D. Hendricks, Matthew Henshaw, John LaPre, JT Moniteau, Christopher Pettus, Adam Rains, Tyson Sereda and Webberly Rattenkraft.

ART BY VISHNU SHYAMALA PRASAD

Tenebrous Ramblings

by Romana Lockwood

Is it you?
    It is you.
    I know it is you.
    My readers.
    Bastards! Bastards! I am poisoned, or somehow otherwise stricken! What have you done to me? A spell? A curse? Why would you cause me these agonies? What motivation could you possibly have? I am elderly! Innocent! My money is tied up in investments, my assets non-liquid, my antiques cursed!
    If left alone, I harm no one! I keep myself to myself, keep my own counsel, mind my business, keep my hands and nose out of the lives of my inferiors!
    No! I will not hear that! It is *not* Rowena, and it is *not* Gert and it is *not* Roberta! How dare you attempt to implicate my doppelgängers! They are very far from here and even if they know of me it is only in blurred and distorted dreams—they are designed, in any event, to wish me only well and never harm, should they discover me at all! Which they will not and have not and how dare you invoke their names without kneeling and bowing your heads!
    I know it is you!
    You win! I will do what you ask of me, damn you. Silence! Silence! What is it you are trying to provoke me to do? Why won't you speak? Oh! My tongue tastes bleach even through its numbness! Bastards! Bastards!
    I know it is you, my readers.
    Ha! *Ha!* I will address you in my column! That's what I am doing now! In my chair, tapping at the keys, pummeling them, cracking them, splitting my nails, bruising my fingertips!
    Oh! So now you blind me? Steal sight from my very eyes?
    Nice try!
    I know the typewriter keys! The home keys have upraised ridges on them! You didn't count on that, did you? You're probably hunt-and-peckers! Little peckers! Little wretched, diseased, gnarled peckers! Abject, withered, *bruised* peckers from which even your wives turn away in horror and revulsion! I'm sorry! I'm sorry! It hurts! It *hurts*!
    I take it back! Okay? *Okay?!*
    I know it is you, my readers!
    I don't know your stupid names! I don't know your loathsome faces, your constellations of pores, yet more dull,

unimaginative variations on the same facial features that have for centuries blighted the front of the damned human head! But you are the only souls to whom I speak, the only ones who could find me! The only ones who could care enough to try to hurt me!

Don't tell me it was the city! I know it wasn't the city! I am revered here. I am an institution! A fixture! A luminary! A record-keeper! If not for me, so much would be forgotten! They wouldn't hurt me, not even if I inadvertently revealed a secret or two. No! They protect me! They will get you! They will find you, and you will pay!

Charlton! Where is my Charlton? CHARLTON! Oh, thank the dickens, here he is, his tooth rubs my toe, and he slides his body along the length of my calf.

If you harm Charlton, even your dead family members I will reawaken to make sure they all over again wish they had never been born and wish even more fervently that they hadn't been reborn! The pain you visit upon me now will be cast upon them a thousandfold plus six! This I promise!

You would exploit my fears and use them against me? I fear not only pain. I fear turn of the century farm equipment; words with u-l-c in them, in that order; the spaces between shutters and walls, one-legged spiders; adults who affect the speech cadences of toddlers; epoxies, emulsifiers, and elastomers. Throw them all at me: your one-horse disc harrows; your gulches, mulches, and ulcers; your narrow, shadowy spaces; your pacifier-stifled man-children; your polyester resins, DATEMs, and styrene-butadiene block copolymers. I will not shrink back; I will not retreat; I will not hide. I have friends in liminal spaces. I have Mr. Buttercup on my side. I have Dark David and Evasive James and Crazy Michael, and they owe me, and they know it.

So, I take it back. I will not do what you ask of me. I will not accede to your demands, spoken, unspoken, hinted at, or disseminated throughout my dreams! I will hunt each one of you down, tear the book from your hands, pull out the pages and jam them into your nostrils and set them aflame. I will then leave you to Mr. Buttercup's caprices, to Dark David's yellow-tinged fangs, to Evasive James's torture quizzes, to Crazy Michael's game of Sticks.

You *readers*. You scum. You pull the words from my brain across space, across time, read them to yourselves in your heads as though they were your own. You read them in a toddler's voice. You underline them with your sad pencils, highlight the passages you deem memorable in your atrocious pastels.

You want to *be* me. Take over. Push me down the porch steps and kick me down the front walk to the road, where your cohorts will bag my head in coarse burlap, pull me into their Black Mariah, drive me to my fate; you want to wake in my bed, plunder my weekly pill organizer, hear the clickety-clack of the typewriter keys, the fractured beat of an epileptic drummer, rip from me my experience without having lived it, without paying a single psychic shilling, without...

My weekly pill organizer! Have I taken my Thursday pills? I don't think that I have. Wait. Wait. Here. Here. Here.

I am sorry, my readers, my silent confidants, my patient and forgiving friends. I take it back. My vision is regained, my pain abates; all is where and as it should be. I haven't had a spell such as this since I was a teenager. Be glad you weren't near me then when I was at full strength. Best keep your distance now, to be safe.

Until next time.

ART BY Æ TRUEMAN

Halogen Sky

Wendy N. Wagner

WE HAD BEEN driving for more than ten hours when the dog vomited a thin stream of yellow gruel down my wife's shoulder. Nancy made the sound a branch makes just before it breaks. The dog whined and strained toward me for comfort as I dove for my purse, searching for my stash of napkins. But no amount of napkins could help the stench of rancid meat and cat turds steaming up the interior of the car.

"Fuck this," Nancy said and swung the car off onto the next crossroad. Its barely two lanes stretched into the empty sagebrush, the road blackly new in the endless nothing of arid plain. Even the dull orange of sunset couldn't add color to this wasteland of dust and rock.

"Are you sure this is a good idea?" I asked, and she shot me one of her Bad Looks, teeth set, nostrils flexed.

"I'm going to find a hotel." Her voice hitched a little, and I felt a spear of guilt. Nancy hated hotels, really hated them, and the dog's nausea was my fault for slipping her a treat two miles earlier, Nancy's tiredness my fault, this whole trip my fault. If I had only learned to drive, or better yet, refused to visit my parents in their apocalyptic bunker, we'd be happily at home, cuddled on the couch in front of the Criterion collection. If only we'd gotten on the road half an hour earlier, before a freak landslide closed the interstate, dumping us onto a string of highways even Google had forgotten about.

"I don't know if there are—"

Her hand sliced through the air, cutting me off. "Didn't you see the sign?"

"I haven't seen a hint of civilization since we got on this highway," I began, but then we topped one of those barely perceptible desert rises, and I saw the little town ahead, or at least one of those clusters of commerce that sometimes spring up alongside highways. An array of thirty-foot-tall signs bristled along the edges of this one narrow road: Popeye's, McDonald's, LaQuinta Inn, Chik-fil-A. A Chevron boasted a Subway and a DQ under one roof. Everything looked freshly painted and clean, all the promise of America with none of the litter.

"They must be expanding the highway or something?" Nancy asked, irritation replaced with curiosity. She glanced over at me, grinning. "Just imagine being the first person to sleep on one of those Hilton hotel beds they're always advertising."

Our friends Erik and Rita had liked their bed at the Hilton so much they got the mattress information from the front desk and ordered a new one when they got home. Of course, they'd been visiting a luxury resort in Hawaii, not a travel hub at the ass-end of Washington. I wasn't sure even truck drivers passed through this place. The pavement looked untouched, the Platonic form of new development.

We didn't pass another car as we rolled downhill into town. After fighting traffic for hours after the interstate disaster, it should have felt good, but the wrongness seeped into the car like the dust. Two narrow strips of green grass bordered the road, as if someone hoped to add a dose of cheer to the desert landscape. I imagined that come Christmas time, the same misguided fool would hang lights and put up some inflatable Santas. The grass would probably be dead by that time.

The stop light came as a surprise, but we stopped and waited our turn for the road. To my left, a Starbucks was clearly still under construction. The dog whined again. She hated being stuck in the car. A tinkling of light piano came from somewhere around the Starbucks' drive-thru lane.

"Did you turn on the radio?" Nancy asked.

"Of course not." I lowered the window a crack, glad for the break in the puke-stink. The music grew louder, bottled jazz piano and acoustic guitar. "It's definitely coming from outside."

She rolled down her own window, risking the ire of her dust allergy. Her nose crinkled. "Is it 'The Girl from Ipanema'?"

"I love that song. It sounds so happy, but the words are so sad."

"You would." She chuckled, and the light changed. The music continued, though, the girl swaying seductively from streetlight to streetlight as we rolled slowly forward. Or so I assumed—there was no change in the volume of the song and no Doppler effect.

We passed a darkened Best Western, the lines in its lot so freshly painted they glowed blue in the twilight shadows. I rubbed my arms, even though the windows were letting in ninety-degree heat. "When you caught the sign, was there a name for this place?"

"Nope, just the blue gas-food-lodging sign. I figured you'd know where we were."

I hesitated, trying to remember some of the trips my father had made us take during his Sunday Drives phase. He'd hold his face in this rictus of fake happiness, more and more teeth showing the farther from home we got. My mother sat in the front seat, unspeaking, eyes fixed on the road as she steadily smoked a pack of cigarettes. My little brother would lay on the floor, trying to breathe from the only narrow ribbon of clean air as I pressed my cheek to the window, crying to myself.

"We only made it out here once," I admitted. "It's so far out of the way, going around the nuclear reservation like this. My dad used to say it was like the US military stuck a pry bar in reality and tore a hole for all their secrets."

"Not creepy at all," Nancy said as we turned into the driveway of a Comfort Travels Inn. The light in the lobby came on as we pulled into the loading zone. I shot Nancy a look, but she was scraping vomit off her shoulder. The dog sat up and gave a single, hollow bark.

"I'll take Molly for a pee if you'll check us in," I suggested.

"Sure, sure." She waved me out of the car and dug under the seat for her phone-wallet.

I opened the back door. "Come on, girl."

Our shepherd mix blinked her one blue, one brown eye at me, and then wobbled a little as she climbed down from the backseat. When she shook herself, tufts of brown and white fur flew everywhere, and her ears bounced like they had springs inside. I had to give her a treat for being so cute.

"Come on, girl," I repeated, urging her toward the green ribbon at the side of the road. We both stopped for stretch breaks, the long drive sliding away as we unwound our way across the cooling black parking lot. The smell of warm plastic wafted off the green. "Fake. Nice."

The dog took a step onto the pseudo-turf and froze. I gave her leash a tiny tug, and she lowered her head and tail, sidling toward the car.

"What's wrong, Molly?"

The dog set more of her thirty-five pounds against the leash.

"Well, if you don't have to pee, you don't have to pee." I let her steer me off the grass. Glancing up, I noticed there were no other cars in the parking lot, and the top half of the four-story hotel was entirely dark. "Nice of them to conserve energy, I guess."

I tried to give Molly a little jog around the lot, but she kept darting toward the car, pawing at the door. It took an entire handful of treats to get her inside the hotel.

The lobby smelled of fresh paint and industrial glue. Efforts had been made to create a welcoming interior, but the rigid gray couches squaring off around a glass coffee table managed only "discount corporate." A set of shelves boasting travel supplies stood empty save for a bottle of Advil and a tube of toothpaste—not in the box.

I went to the counter, where a lone employee buried their face in the computer monitor. I stood there a long moment while they ignored me. Keystrokes echoed in the empty room, as did the soft sound of my throat clearing.

"Hello?"

The person at the computer tilted their head an infinitesimal degree toward me but said nothing.

"Did a woman just check in? My height? Short red hair?"

"Mmm-hmm." The keyboard emitted another burst of clacking.

I took a deep breath. "Do you know where she went?"

The hotel employee sighed and extended an arm toward the far side of the lobby. "Room 113."

I noticed now a hallway opening beside the elevator bank, its gray carpet made gloomier by a half-dead fluorescent light. "Thanks."

They said nothing. When I glanced back at them from the entrance of the hallway, ready to make some kind of irritated and perhaps snarky comment, I felt the words dry on my tongue. Beneath a squared bob with fluffy black bangs, the person behind the counter had my face. My wire-rimmed glasses. My slightly connected eyebrows. My wide mouth and square chin. Even a scar on the upper lip, a white accent mark springing off the top of the cupid's bow.

They turned around and vanished into what must have been an office. Molly whimpered.

The fluorescent light above me crackled, the gloom flickering from full dark to absurdly bright and then back again. I made my way to Room 113, whose door stood open. Nancy had gotten us one with two queens, both made up with comforters the color of unsorted laundry. The entertainment center, typically occupied by a television, stretched out barren and empty, with only a reproduction of Monet's *Water Lilies* propped against the wall to distract the eye from the décor. Everything felt as gray as the sagebrush outside the window.

"There you are," Nancy said, standing at the sink in only her bra. She scrubbed the tiny bar of soap over the shirt soaking in the basin. "I was thinking we could grab a bite before we bring our suitcases in from the car."

"Yeah, sure." I pulled my phone from my purse and sat down on the bed. "Let me just call my folks first." But my phone warned me we were too far from any kind of service area to make a call.

"There's no Wi-Fi either," Nancy complained. "Can I borrow your cardigan?"

I shrugged off the sweater and watched her button it, the reverse of a strip tease, but still pleasing. "Maybe the McDonald's will have one. I saw one across the street that looked open."

We settled Molly onto the second bed and headed back outside. No one attended the front desk.

"Did you notice the way the check-in person looked just like me?"

Nancy paused in front of the counter, pocketing a peppermint from the cup beside the register. "I guess they had your same glasses."

"And my chin."

She shook her head, walking faster toward the exit. "You're much cuter."

For a moment I thought the lobby doors would stand impenetrable against our exit, but Nancy's room key let us outside. Night had collapsed across the desert, and now only the white glare of the halogen streetlights illuminated the world. "The Girl from Ipanema" continued to play.

"I'm surprised more of these businesses aren't open," Nancy said as we crossed the street. "I guess they're just waiting until the highway construction is complete?"

"I guess." A breeze had come up in the night, and I regretted giving Nancy my sweater. The nubs of goose flesh made my skin too tight, and the cooling plastic grass needled the bottoms of my thin canvas sneakers.

A constellation of fast food options ran along this side of the road, the promise of sameness written in their bland, boxy shapes and their trademarked lights, the commonplace of American travel. I had seen mile after mile of such offerings in our drive today. Wherever asphalt had been spread, the traveler could root themselves, at home even when separated from their physical abode. My body, held tight and still within the confines of my seatbelt and bucket seat, could probably be convinced via taste and smell that I had never left Portland.

Except there were no smells here besides the electric scent of sagebrush, underpinned with the faint iron scent of granulated basalt. The exterior lights still glowed, but every lobby stood empty and dark. Only the McDonald's sent out a glow of welcome.

The jazz piano grew louder as we crossed the empty drive-thru lane and made for the door. Beneath the restaurant's awning, the song's volume rose to brain-piercing levels, the singer's voice burning through my ear canals and buzzing my mastoid bones.

One person stood behind the counter, their hair a squared yet puffy bob with straight bangs and wire-rimmed glasses. I grabbed Nancy's arm and raised my eyebrows. She made an amazed face and then turned back to the counter.

"Hello again." Nancy smiled and glanced up at the menu. I hadn't eaten at a McDonald's in probably ten years, but the selection looked approximately the same.

The person at the counter said nothing. They had taken off their red blazer and now wore a black polo shirt with the McDonald's logo on the clavicle. The collar of their white button-down shirt looked awkwardly crammed into the neckline of the polo. I noticed a pimple at the corner of their left eyebrow that mirrored the one at the corner of my right.

I tried to smile and act as friendly as I would in any other restaurant situation. "Can I get a quarter pounder and a green salad with ranch dressing?"

"And can I get a Big Mac with a medium Diet Coke, a large order of fries, and a cherry pie?"

"That will be $9.50" The person at the register hadn't pushed any of its buttons.

"Great!" Nancy pulled a twenty out of her back pocket. The worker gave her the change and turned toward the kitchen. "Hey—can I get my drink?"

The person vanished into the back of the house. There were no lights on back there, and no warm, golden smells of frying food.

I grabbed Nancy's arm again and pulled her into my side. "This is really weird. And I can't believe you don't think that person looks like me. Like, we could be twins."

Nancy snorted. "Jill, I'm not even sure that person is a woman. You're being paranoid because you're sure your parents will be pissed at you for not getting to their house tonight. But I *will* be amazed if this weird worker gives us anything like what we ordered."

The counter worker reappeared with a plastic bag, which they dropped on the end of the counter. They hesitated a moment and pulled a stack of napkins out of their back pocket, which they piled beside the food. "We're closing now."

"Okay, I guess we'll take this to go—"

"We're closing," they repeated, and vanished into the back. The lights went out.

"Jesus Christ," Nancy grumbled. The glow from the neighboring Taco Bell was just bright enough for us to find our way to the doors. She swore a few more times as we crossed the street and retrieved our luggage from the trunk of our car.

The tires on Nancy's carry-on squeaked as she dragged it behind her. The plastic bag swung beside my leg, something solid hitting my thigh every alternate step. Nancy paused at the door, reaching for the key card in her back pocket.

"Did I ever tell you why I hate hotels so much?"

I shook my head, but she was busy with the door. The squeaky wheel echoed inside the lobby. The lights had lowered while we were out, and now the gray couches and empty shelves sat in shadows, their edges undefined. It looked better this way, less new, less haphazard. We could have been in any highway-facing hotel in any stretch of flyover country. The fluorescent light at the mouth of our hallway sent out a surge of white light.

"When I was a little girl, my parents took me on a trip to visit my aunt and uncle. They lived in Sacramento, so it was a long drive. We had to stay in a motel someplace along the way. Medford, maybe? Redding?" She shook her head. "It doesn't matter."

The wheels of her carry-on caught on the seam between the lobby's fake hardwood and the carpeted hallway. I nudged it forward with my toe.

"As a treat, they sent me to the drink machine to get us each a can of pop. I felt so grown-up, carrying those three one-dollar bills in my hand, trying not to crumple them. But when I stepped into the hallway, I wasn't sure which direction to go—left or right, they both looked the same. And when I started walking, the hallway started to stretch." She stopped and gave me one of her Very Serious Looks. "I don't mean like it *seemed* to grow. It really did stretch, Jill. It got longer and longer, and the faster I walked, the faster it grew. I started running, but it didn't matter. Door after door after door. I ran so long. I thought I'd never see my parents again."

"That must have been terrifying."

She started walking again: squeak, squeak, squeak. Thud against my leg. We passed room 104.

"My parents found me sitting in the hallway two doors from our room, crying. I still had the dollars." She stopped to look over her shoulder. Cleared her throat. "Whenever I'm inside a hotel, I can feel it." We stopped in front of our own room, and she dug in her jeans for the keycard. The look on her face, deeply focused and yet somehow absent made me think of my mother on those long Sunday drives.

"Feel what?"

Nancy kicked open the door, and we had to spend a minute soothing Molly. She did her usual anxiety dancing, throwing her furry body against our waists, licking our hands and elbows, desperate for reconnection. I gave her an extra hug, burying my face in her shaggy head fur, which had its own unique perfume of spice and Fritos. A good stink.

I didn't even want Nancy to answer my question now, but as she dumped the plastic bag of food out on the bed she said very quietly: "There's a part of me that really believes every hotel is that hotel, no matter what it says on the sign."

I put my hand on her shoulder. She didn't put her hand on top of mine like she normally would have.

"Hey, there are Oreos!" Nancy grinned like this was all a fun adventure, so Molly and I sat down on the bed to better see what we'd gotten: three ham sandwiches wrapped in plastic, two bottles of water, and an entire package of Oreo cookies.

We let Molly have one of the sandwiches because it had been one of those days, and besides, she wasn't allowed Oreos.

I woke in the night to sound of Molly's collar jingling, her feet scuffing on the carpet as she made frantic circles at the door. My neck ached from the too-thin pillow, and my mouth tasted like Oreos and ashes, despite brushing and flossing. I really needed to start bringing my electric toothbrush with me when I traveled, but I hated the idea of anything happening to such an expensive tool.

"Molly?" Nancy mumbled, rolling onto her side.

"I got it." I jammed my feet into my shoes and found my cardigan where Nancy had draped it over the Monet. Now that I was up, Molly had stopped circling. She made a little snuffle as I dug in Nancy's jeans pocket to find the keycard. Nancy's story was starting to surface inside my sleepy brain, the weirdness of it and the entire day making me hesitate, one hand on the door chain. When I opened the door, I half expected the hallway to stretch into infinity. It looked normal enough, although the light at the end of the hallway had given up, leaving me to walk in gloom all the way to the lobby. Molly walked so close to me her fur sparked static on my pajama bottoms.

"It's okay, girl," I whispered, fumbling the key across the reader and opening the door.

It was brighter outside, the streetlights and safety lamps in the parking lot burning so brightly it made my eyes sting. Molly loped across the pavement, headed for the grass strip beside the road. I had to run to catch up and then grab for her collar The dog-heated nylon pressed into my fingers, a contrast to the cold night air. I turned my face up to the sky, but the brilliance of the artificial lighting had bleached the darkness out of it. There were no moon, no stars, only that sick halogen white.

A breeze blew the smell of bacon toward us. I shut my eyes and drew it in, mouth watering. If only I'd grabbed my purse, I could have picked us up some fourth meal—

My eyes shot open as I felt Molly's collar slip out of my grip. "Molly, come back!"

But she was running, running like I'd never seen her run before. I tried to run after her, but the grass ripped beneath my feet, dropping me into the mud. Car horns shrieked. Brakes squealed. Someone shouted. I got to my feet, but there were too many cars, too many lights, I couldn't see her anywhere.

"Molly!" I screamed. A part of me knew the impossible had happened, that I ought to be standing next to an empty road in an empty corner of the

Washington desert, not chasing my dog through a crowded street that could have been Seattle or Portland or fucking Beijing.

"Molly," I breathed, and now the world spun in a slow circle around me, the logos of a dozen franchises blurring, voices shouting, some of them angry, some trying to help, some simply hungry, so very hungry. And then, just as I was stumbling onto the road, trying to follow Molly wherever she had gone, I heard it, the one, the voice that had been running beneath them all, the quietly buoyant voice of the girl from Ipanema.

It came from behind me, so loud it made my head hurt. I whipped around to face the hotel. The world went silent. The hotel hunched in its asphalt skirts, the lamp posts in the parking lot humming their barely perceptible electrical hum. There sat our car, and there stretched the desert. The wind picked up again, cold and mineral and smelling only of sagebrush. When I glanced over my shoulder, I was alone, the grass strip fake again, the world gone empty in every direction. Wherever Molly had gone, it wasn't there any longer.

I found the keycard in my cardigan pocket and went back inside the lobby. I stood alone. I didn't know how to tell Nancy what had happened to our dog.

The light at the end of the hallway buzzed angrily, sparking white. Then it snapped off, the light beyond it going with it. Darkness filled this end of the hallway, save for a milky square on the carpet where the door to Room 104 stood open.

I didn't want to walk past it, but there was no alternative. When they crossed the line from darkness to white, my toes shrank inside my sneakers. Inside the room, a child sniffled.

"Hello?" It came out a whisper. It took all my will power turn my neck and shoulders to face the white void of the doorway.

Beyond the opening stretched nothing. Not darkness, not outer space: nothing. Only the pale, lifeless glow of some vast halogen bulb, its light pushing into our world like a pry bar wriggling into a crack. It breathed out an emptiness that drained the life from my legs. My butt bounced as I hit the ground. A faint scent of menthol cigarettes rose from the carpet, like a memory washed and re-washed until the context came unwoven. The light breathed on. A little girl cried, lost and lonely, but it was so far off in the distance I wasn't really sure I heard it. Maybe it was the sound of nothing. The sound of broken light fixtures. The true language of hotels and roadside places.

The light burned hotter and whiter behind my eyes. The pores of my skin tore open, hungrily sucking me into my own self. The hollow spaces in my bones expanded, cracking and bursting into pain, into burning nothing. Screaming, I spun in the empty places of my body, the empty places in my life. My mother stubbed a cigarette back into fire. Nancy walked backward out of a restaurant, her introductory email unsending. A man in green fatigues jammed a post-hole digger into the Earth and pierced its core. A bell rang on a counter beside a dish of peppermints.

The door swung closed. I found myself on my side, tears turning to crust on the side of my face. The carpet's cheap polyester threads cut into the bare skin of my ankles and cheek.

I made myself get up and walk to our room on aching, jellied legs. For a second the keycard refused to work, but then I turned it another way, and the reader flashed its green light and let me push down the handle.

"Nancy?"

But of course, she said nothing. The gray beds lay untouched, their corners square. A painting of a lighthouse hung above a flatscreen TV. Beside it, a bottle of Advil and a tube of toothpaste, half-flattened, sat beside a stack of clothing: clean underthings, white sports socks, a pair of khakis, a button-down shirt, a red blazer. I reached for the Advil and took four. When I pressed my hand to my face, my fingers smelled like a dog, although I couldn't remember why.

I thought about taking another Advil. The alarm went off on the clock beside the bed.

I got dressed, although I hesitated a second before I put on the red blazer. My hands shook as I did up the buttons. When the alarm squawked again, I realized there was no time to brush my teeth if I didn't want to be late for my shift.

As I walked to the front desk, I could already see guests waiting for me to check them in, the lobby music tinkling quietly beneath their murmurs. It was "The Girl from Ipanema," of course. It was always "The Girl from Ipanema."

I welcomed each and every person to the Comfort Travels Inn, my smile burning like halogen.

Twenty-Nine Palms in Reverse

Daniel Braum

TWENTY-NINE PALMS, CALIFORNIA.
Yuli isn't here for the reason Noam thinks.
He pulls the key from the ignition and exhales, his other hand still gripping the wheel. The line of sandy brown earth and gray exposed rock snaking its way through the Joshua trees and cactus and brush all the way to the mountain ridge in the distance barely qualifies as a dirt road. Yuli opens the rental jeep's door and dry desert heat hits, the hot, fragrant air overcoming artificially cool and sterile. She secures her camera strap around her neck. The jeep's engine is still rumbling, unhappy about the steep, jagged incline Noam just gunned his way up. She didn't think he had it in him.

He's spotted something.

"Don't tell me," Yuli says. "I want to try-"

"Why bring your personal spotter then?"

She shushes him by blowing him a kiss the way she always does, then flips her hair and searches the ridge for bighorn sheep through her long lens. There are none. Movement in the corner of her vision catches her attention. Too tall for a bighorn. A person? Someone walking? She can't zero in. She searches the stillness between the jeep and the ridge. It's a prehistoric landscape of surreal rock formations and ancient twenty to thirty foot Joshua Trees, their crooked limbs towering over patches of barrel cacti and silvery bush-like cholla, undisturbed by tourists and climbers from LA. There are no other vehicles. We're probably outside the park, she thinks. She lowers the camera.

Canine prints and tracks of a bird, probably a road runner or quail, are in the earth before her, a story of passage in the dried-up evidence of a flash flood. Then she sees what Noam stopped for. A tortoise. Crossing the "road" only a few yards away. Its domed shell scarred with healed over cracks. From its size, she guesses it might be even older than the Joshua Trees. She picks it up, turns it around, and places it in the safety of the rock formation from where it began its crossing. She glances at Noam leaning on the jeep in his jeans and white tee, as he's scanning the ridge in the distance, looking cool as a cucumber with his week old scruff and mop of unruly brown hair and his expression unaware of her and focused on the landscape before them. She finds him—and the whole moment—beautiful, a frame of a 1950's movie come to life.

"The first time I came out here I was still in school," Yuli says.

"We were all such dopes. I don't remember having any water and was probably wearing sneakers. This guy who was with us, he wasn't bright at all. We all thought he was stripping to pay his way through school. He yells from up ahead, hey look there's a big boa sleeping up here. I found a boa! I knew enough about snakes to know there are no boas out here, but the first thing my mind thinks is wow, he's found a boa and it's probably someone's lost pet, and we have to save it. So, we catch up with him, and I stick my face in the rocks where he's pointing and yeah, there *is* a big ass snake coiled up sleeping in there. Only it's not a boa, it's a six foot plus thick, thick diamond back rattlesnake-"

"Yuliana. You're doing it again," Noam says.

"Am I?"

Noam nods.

"I am. Sorry. You know, it's just... California is where I started. Where I started being me. I want to show you everything. I want you to know all of me."

"I wish we could be somewhere that's new ground for both of us," Noam says. "That's what couples do."

"I'm taking California back from my past, so it's ours now, too. That's *also* something couples do."

She notices movement again. She was right. Someone *is* way out there at the foot of the ridge. A woman. Dwarfed by the Joshua trees. Slowly walking towards them. Yuli brings her camera to her eye, pushes the lens to the max, trying to zero in, unable to keep the woman in the frame. She zooms out, spotting her briefly before losing her among the ancient trunks.

"And there you go," Noam says.

He's holding the tortoise, its legs moving in the air. He places it on the other side of the dirt path.

"You're not supposed to put them *back*," he says. "You're supposed to help them *cross*."

"Cross? This isn't even a road. This isn't even anywhere," Yuli says. She walks to him and kisses his cheek. "Is my spotter getting grumpy? Need some water and AC?"

"No, I'm... not sure we're in the right place. I don't think this is the right ridge. There's supposed to be a pool of run off. A watering hole. Maybe we shouldn't have gone up that incline."

Noam scans the plain with his binoculars.

"See anything?" Yuli asks.

She's hoping he finds a mountain lion. Steve and Steve from the guest house said they're out here but nearly impossible to spot during the day unless moving. And they won't be moving unless going for water or prey.

"Um, nothing," Noam says after a pause that feels too long.

Before she can ask him what's wrong or tell him to get over himself, she's not sure which, he lowers the binoculars and points.

"Kestrel, fifty feet ahead," he says. "See that Joshua Tree? The one that looks sorta like a windmill?"

"Check. See it."

"Third branch up, halfway to the spiky leaf-tufts at the end. There's a kestrel trying to stuff a dead baby snake in its hollow."

"Oooh, I see it."

The tiny snake, not dead after all, doubles back on itself, lunging with fangs bared.

"Oooh, look at that. You're so good to me."

"Now that's what I like to hear. Don't ever say I don't do anything for you..."

Yuli photographs the snake as it frees itself and falls. She wonders about the pause in Noam's reply. Did he see the woman out there too?

The sun is ready to go down. The big blue open desert sky behind the ridge will soon be filled with color. The kestrel takes flight, its gliding arc the only motion in the windless, natural garden.

There is something kinetic in the stillness. It dawns on her it's been too long since she's felt this connected and alive.

Steve and his husband of the same name designed the guest house themselves, and had it constructed entirely from materials found on their sprawling acreage just inside the border of the National Park. The low building's stone and timber contour is made to resemble the ridge on the horizon behind it and fit in with the natural landscape. Yuli chose it because she hoped Noam would love it.

The four of them finish dinner and sit at the long reclaimed wood table by the big window, granting a perfect view of outside. The Joshua trees are not nearly as tall as the ones from this afternoon.

"Steve's grandfather bought the land decades ago, before the Park was a Park," the Steve who is a former chef says, "So we're literally grandfathered-in around the no-building and living inside the park rules, as Steve likes to say."

"Well, the hippies and climbers always knew Twenty-Nine Palms was the place to be," the other Steve says. He's the one Yuli spoke to when booking and is also a guide. "They knew the LA people and hipsters would one day creep in."

"Which one was your grandfather?" Steve asks as he gathers the plates.

Yuli gazes outside. Dusk is bathing the rock and cactus and ocotillo and all the desert things in shadow. She catches Noam staring too.

"Hmmm, good question," Steve answers. "Give it ten years, no one's gonna recognize this place."

"Change is the only constant, my dear."

"Is it?"

"Our guests don't want to hear us debate and philosophize."

"Quite the contrary," Noam says.

"So, did you find the watering hole and the bighorns?" Steve asks.

"Didn't find the water," Noam says. "We were up that steep part, to where the big Joshua Trees are."

"Oh, you were right there. That's the oldest part of the forest. You're lucky you didn't break an axle."

"Yeah, no signal, you'd be fucked," Steve says carrying the plates to the kitchen.

"Pardon my husband's French. It's almost dark. Say give it an hour then we meet back here for that night walk?"

"Night walk? Deadly scorpions," Steve calls from the kitchen. "I pass."

Yuli finds herself jealous of the giddy, affectionate expression that comes over Steve's face in response to his husband's foolery.

She and Noam bring their gear from the jeep into their room. The entrance into their small, cave-like space is a glass door providing an unobstructed view of the property and the desert beyond.

"We going to unpack or–"

Yuli playfully pushes Noam onto the bed and jumps on him, pulling at their clothes hoping her frenzied kisses will come across as passionate. The connection she felt outside translates to the moment. This is something better than at home. Almost good again, she thinks. She closes her eyes in surrender. An image of the woman walking through the trees is there waiting.

After, lying there naked, catching her breath with him, she can't point to why she feels dissatisfied.

"What?" Noam says.

"You weren't into it, were you? I felt you weren't."

"What? I totally was."

"What were you thinking?" Yuli asks. "Come on where were you?"

"Here. I mean, at one point I felt *you* weren't really here, then I got lost in it all ..."

"Lost in it, huh?"

"I'll show you how into you I am," Noam says. "But we're going to miss the hike."

As they are squirming into their clothes, Yuli is startled by a woman walking towards her, but it is only the reflection from the bedside lamp-glare on the glass.

Steve, the guide, knows every inch of the property. Under the stars and moon the desert is a different kind of gorgeous. Silver leaves, spindly cactus arms and all the rocks and textures take on new color and shape in the light of night and its shadows. Steve does not deliver on his promise of a scorpion for her to shoot, but there are plenty of active long-tailed kangaroo rats scavenging and one rattler that escapes into a burrow after pleasing them with its name-sake warning. Her prize is the tarantula Noam spots on a cactus at the end of the walk near the house.

In the middle of the night, while Noam is sleeping, she returns outside to search for the spider again. The sound of coyotes yipping and barking fills the silence. She is unsure if the pack is coming or going. Noam was right. It was her who wasn't present when they were fucking. She was wondering about the woman out there and envisioning the giant trees lit by stars and all the shades of brown at night in a negative image of the day.

It is not that she doesn't want him, mostly she does. And she thinks she loves him. At least more than she's loved anyone before. The burden is that *this* isn't what she thought being thirty-five would be. She doesn't know what it *should* be and would say fuck off to anyone who tried to tell her. Though there is nothing wrong, she knows her life is not supposed to be the one she is living. She knows this awareness is a dangerous cage to be in and one even more dangerous to wake up in with regret years later. She was not lying. The twin thought of the truth she told Noam is that she is also here to decide if she is going to leave him.

A water droplet lands on her, then another. The cloudless sky empties of rain. She wasn't sure if it ever rained in the desert. She knew it must. Now she knows the truth firsthand. The downpour stops a minute later. She spots the spider on the cactus, touching a droplet beaded on the tip of a thorn with its front legs. She listens for the sound of a flash flood in the canyon she knows must be on the other side of the ridge in the distance.

Instead of following the directions to search for the ridge with the watering hole, Noam guns it up the incline again, and she doesn't protest.

He stops the jeep in nearly the same place as yesterday. Everything has exploded into colors. Yellow, pink, and white cactus blooms. Red ocotillo flowers, silver cholla plump with moisture. The tracks she had seen yesterday in the dried earth have been worn smooth by the rain.

"Can we go out there?" Yuli asks. "Make it to the ridge?"

"I was thinking that too. It's farther than it looks, and there are so many rocks. We shouldn't take a chance with the axle."

"Want to walk it?" she asks.

"Hell yeah. I can spot for boas."

"Very funny."

"I thought you'd think so. Hey, look at me, I'm a stripper. I think I found someone's pet python."

He takes off his shirt and spins it overhead with his finger. His childish display of jealousy is not attractive.

"Ha, ha. Enough. You're gonna get one hell of a sunburn."

"Then take me into the backseat," he says.

He playfully grabs her and pushes her against the jeep. She pushes back harder than they both expected.

"How about we take it easy, Tiger?" she says. "Save it for tonight, and make good use of this daylight instead?"

"Fine," Noam says. "I'll be a good spotter."

She doesn't like that she's lied to him. She knows it's a very bad sign she can't be honest; that he is not man enough to hear about a school day's fling she had over a decade ago. Long before she knew him.

His name was Adam. He was an escort, not a stripper, though he did sometimes bounce at a strip club. They used to come out to the desert, with no money for fancy places. It was just them and the truck and a tent. He wasn't stupid at all. Yeah, he got high too much and talked about a dead end job, but, wow, did they ever click in bed. With Adam she felt like a dance partner, not a plaything. He wrote her stories, made up just for her, using characters from her favorite books and movies.

One night, in the desert under the stars while they were pontificating on life and the people they would become, Adam proclaimed, "I'm not a prostitute. I choose who I'm with," and told her he was only doing it because he was on the run from his life in Nevada. She never asked or found out quite what he meant by that. The next time she went to see him, he was gone. Gone as in his truck wasn't at his place. Gone as in his roommates had moved too. She checked and checked again. No one had even seen him at the club. In the pre-internet age this was disappeared for real. It was just a fling, but the loss of possibility, the loss of the feeling that sex, pleasure, art, and the natural world was what life meant, and what life had in store was a real blow. So much was lost along the way of growing up. She hates she cannot tell Noam this.

They push through the heat towards the ridge. Noam offers her water every few minutes and is a good spotter. There is nothing wrong with the moment, Yuli thinks. The moment is quite pleasant. Noam's sweat slicked olive skin glistens in the sun. The cactus and trees and flowers are unfathomably beautiful. Noam is quiet. Quiet is his default state, and that's okay. She prefers to think it evidences unknowable depths as opposed to there being nothing to him. She knows he values being in the moment and being in strings of moments with her. She hopes there is more to him than this.

She realizes she is looking through a disturbance in the air, a wall of heat-haze giving everything a distorted shimmer. Through the disturbance she sees the woman. They are both walking. With her next step Yuli realizes she is walking toward the woman, and the woman is walking towards her. They are both converging on the disturbance.

With the thought, she feels faint. Noam gently catches her as she stumbles backwards.

"Wow, you're dehydrated," he says. "It happens fast. We have to drink a bottle an hour. I'm feeling it too-"

"I *have* been drinking."

They stand there passing a water bottle back and forth. Yuli can no longer see it, but she can sense where the disturbance was. Its exact place. She can feel the line.

"How much further?" she asks. "I want to go."

"Huh," Noam says.

"I want to keep walking. I want to take some shots."

"Okay," he says.

She expected him to protest. "Aren't you going to ask me?"

"Ask you what?"

"What I'm shooting?"

"You're an artist, Yuli. I trust you. This is me being the crew. I'm on the assist this trip, right?"

"Right."

She looks into the distance hoping to see the woman. She knows it is possible to walk out there and… what? Would they cross paths, what would happen? She feels the faintness coming again.

She thinks she should say something to Noam. He is staring at the ridge, his mouth releasing soft mutterings.

"What are you doing?" she asks.

"Um, just writing," he says.

"Now? What were you writing? You don't write."

"Poems," he says. "And yes, I do."

"I've never seen you."

"True. They're in my head. I keep them there."

"Really? You don't write them down?"

"Maybe someday. Maybe the ones that stay with me long enough."

"I never knew you did that," she says.

Maybe the reason to be a couple isn't to know everything about each other, she thinks. Maybe it is what will be seen together. The uncharted ground, like he said yesterday.

"I want to go back to the room now," she says.

"You sure? Daylight's burning."

"Yeah, I have a job for my personal spotter that needs immediate attention."

For the first time in as long as she can remember, she is certain about how she feels.

The sex is the best she can remember, their kisses approaching the lost magic. Something Adam once said to her jumps into her mind. Life is converging and intertwined lines, he'd said. The tough part is figuring out whose story is whose. Is your direction your own? Are you the lead in your story? Or a side player in someone else's? Or are all we all nothing at all?

"So, his name was Adam," Noam says.

"Who?"

"The stripper?"

"What? Why would you say that? How do you know that?"

"You were calling his name."

"I was not. Was I?"

"You never told me his name. His name is Adam. How else would I know?"

Yuli doesn't know what to do, so she storms out the door and walks around the house to the main entrance. Steve, the chef, is there setting the table and having a cigarette.

"Everything okay, boss?" he asks.

"Um, yeah, sure just came to see if I could beg a smoke."

"You can't. I'm not supposed to, and you caught me. Steve's out getting bread. Oh, no, you are *not* okay. What's wrong?"

"How long have you been with Steve? Was it always bliss between you two?"

"Wow, that's a personal question for before dinner. Let's see, you're in my home and sure, I can add therapist to the many lines on my resume. So. No, it wasn't."

"How did you do it? I mean, how did you make it work?"

"I've learned that everything is a choice. There's no magic to love and staying together. No formula either. When it comes down to it, it is a choice to come together and when things get rough to stay together, or not. Everyone I've ever asked—I asked a lot before Steve and I worked it all out—says the same. Fight for him. Drag him to you or to counseling or whatever. Do whatever you've got to do."

"Right," she says. "You're right, thank you. I shouldn't have run out on him."

"Don't mention it." He holds up his smoke. "And by that I really mean don't mention it."

Yuli's ashamed, so she decides to take a walk on the trail they were on last night to cool down and clear her head before going back to work it all out with Noam.

On the path she comes across a tortoise crossing to a patch of cactus, going the opposite way of the one she saw yesterday. It is identical in size; she wonders if it is the same reptile. She contemplates helping it across. As she kneels to lift it, she sees its shell is free of cracks and scars. She sees no reason to do anything other than watch it as it ambles into the rocks and brush.

An hour later she returns to the room. The jeep and Noam are gone. She runs to the main house.

"Hey, where'd Noam go?"

"Don't know," Steve, the guide, says.

"Can I borrow your truck?"

"We're not supposed to-"

"Yes," Steve, the chef, says and tosses her a ring of keys.

Yuli knows where to go. Where else would Noam go?

As she speeds on the desert road flanked by Joshua Trees, she wonders is there another Yuli racing toward her? Is it possible that she is the other and out there, there is a Yuli this never happened to? A Yuli who never knew doubt?

When she reaches the incline, she guns it, like Noam. The truck bottoms out and lurches, she thinks it is going to flip. It drags on something with a terrible clack of metal on rock, the death knell of an axle, for sure. The truck loses power and slides back down the incline.

Yuli gets out and decides to climb. Hand over hand. There are so many rocks. It takes her a few minutes to cover what in the jeep had taken seconds.

Coyotes are yipping and barking nearby. This time she knows they are leaving for a night of raiding the dumpsters and open cans of Twenty-Nine Palms. Something else is out in the dusk with her. A throaty feline gurgle that can only be a mountain lion breaks the quiet. She's without her camera, without her phone, and feels naked instead of scared shitless to be close to a predatory big cat she cannot see. She revels in the thrill.

Yuli pulls her way to the top and spots Noam. He's already walked far and is nearing the disturbance before the ridge. His lean form is dwarfed by the old trees and the heat-mirage wavering in the air before him. Is there another him out there on the other side walking towards him? Is she going to look through it and see another man walking towards her Noam? Is she going to look and see that the woman walking towards her is another her?

Their rental jeep is still running. The door is open. Noam's left his boots and his shirt. Something compels her to copy him and to take off her boots. The dry earth feels good. She steps in a moist swath of ground, a place where a flash flood passed. She is making tracks. Tracks that will remain for who knows how long until they're washed away by the next rain.

When she reaches the wavering, will she walk through it and keep walking, and nothing will happen? Will she switch places with the woman? Will they pass through each other? Will she even know? Noam is right there. A few more steps, and he's there.

Yuli sees the woman. The face, the body are visually identical to hers, but Yuli knows the woman is not her. Some spirit, some feeling, the toll of the paths she's walked through the years and the weight of burden's she's carried are absent.

She sees the wavering and can see through it at the same time. One more step and Noam will reach it. One more second and she'll know what will happen to him. She'll know what is in store for her too.

She senses presences all around her. Animals. All the animals living here. Birds, coyotes, insects. Each one registers as noise in the quiet. She spots a gray coyote camouflaged in a pile of rock. Another at the brown foot of a Joshua Tree trunk. She becomes aware of another and another. There is an entire pack among the trees and rocks. She sees a roadrunner in the distance. Hawks. Lizards. A tortoise emerging from its burrow. Kangaroo rats and hares leaving the cover of brush. A scorpion uncurls itself from its hiding spot at the base of a barrel cactus. She becomes aware of all of them with a speed and certainty Noam could never match.

Bighorn sheep are watching from the ridge. Are their instincts to avoid danger keeping them away or calling them? From somewhere nearby the mountain lion releases a long yowl, powerful enough to resonate in her sternum. The hot air is full of the herbal mix of everything that grows here. Wind sweeps through the dusk. Yuli's mind fills with the image of a palm tree, not with roots beneath ground, but another trunk and fronds burrowing into an inverted world that looks almost the same as here, but where she hopes things are not the same as here at all.

ART BY JULIE BLANKENSHIP

THE DEVIL'S JUST SITTING THERE LAUGHING : THE UNCANNY AMERICAN LANDSCAPES OF TERRENCE MALICK'S *BADLANDS* AND *DAYS OF HEAVEN*

Gwendolyn Kiste

A plague of locusts. A legendary murder spree. Fires that obliterate homes—and all the hopes that go with them.

While often lauded among cinema fans, Terrence Malick's work is rarely given its due through the lens of horror and the weird, despite having clear elements of both. In particular, his first two feature films—1973's *Badlands* and 1978's *Days of Heaven*—are rife with unsettling and haunting images that evoke classic ghost stories, a decidedly Gothic aesthetic, tales of true crime, and even occasionally cosmic horror.

The American Dream, Dissected
In his highly lauded debut, *Badlands*, Terrence Malick introduces us to Kit and Holly, played with disarming coolness by a young Martin Sheen and Sissy Spacek, a pair of small-town kids from South Dakota. Loosely based on the Starkweather homicides, the two of them take the juvenile delinquency of the 1950s to the next level—and then some. But while earlier outlaws Bonnie and Clyde were high-minded enough to want to derail authority on behalf of working class people, Kit and Holly have no such great aspirations. In fact, they seem to have few aspirations at all, as they sleepwalk through their lives. In their world, committing murder is almost as banal as

twirling a baton, the very childlike activity Holly's practicing when Kit first spots her in her front yard.

Days of Heaven, on the other hand, is less horrifying on the surface, concerning itself with an ill-fated love triangle on the prairie. However, it soon proves to be just as tragic and remote as its counterpart, *Badlands*. Set primarily in the Texas panhandle in the 1910s, Abby and Bill (Brooke Adams and Richard Gere) are two lovers on the run, the same as Kit and Holly. Only instead of a murder spree, they end up on a vast wheat farm where they pose as brother and sister and ultimately devise a scheme to marry off Abby to the wealthy yet lonely farmer who runs the property (Sam Shepard). Observing it all is Bill's actual sister, Linda, played by a brilliant teenage Linda Manz, who's relegated to the sidelines of the story yet serves as its emotional epicenter nonetheless.

Despite the bleakness of his characters' circumstances, Malick's films are nothing if not stunning. The influence of American art permeates *Days of Heaven*, in particular the work of Andrew Wyeth and Edward Hopper[1]. When Abby first meets the Farmer, she emerges upon the pastoral scene like the figure in Wyeth's *Christina's World*. The Farmer's house, referred to as the Belvedere, is a work of art unto itself. It lingers like a specter over the wheat fields and is instantly reminiscent of Edward Hopper's famed painting *House by the Railroad*. With nothing around it but open fields and open skies, it seems as if the house is doomed to be haunted, if not by a literal ghost, then by the land itself.

(It's worth noting that Hopper's *House by the Railroad* inspired not only the Farmer's home in *Days of Heaven*, but also a far more famous cinematic abode: Norman Bates' Gothic hilltop mansion in *Psycho*[2]. This serves as yet another horror connection in Malick's work—one that was probably not lost on the director).

But the horror connections don't end there. There's something particularly strange and even spooky in the Farmer's countenance. Not only does his property serve as a nexus for the film, a rural haunted house that seems more like a wax museum than a cozy home, but the Farmer rarely speaks, and he's never even given a name. Instead, he looms over the film like something ethereal, a figure both there and not there.

---

[1] Almendros. "Photographing *Days of Heaven*."
[2] Edward-Hopper.org. "*House by the Railroad*."

Early on, the audience, along with Bill, learns that the Farmer is terminally ill with an unspecified malady, thereby imbuing his entire screen presence with an elegiac quality. Actor Sam Shepard even went so far as to describe his character as "a ghost,"[3] a description that only enhances the already haunting qualities of the performance. In his character, death has come to the prairie, and, by the end, no one will be spared from its whirlwind.

(In an initial version of the script, Shepard's character was more fleshed out, boasting a fully realized backstory and even given a proper name: Chuck[4]. Indeed, all the characters were given richer and more complex backgrounds in the first draft of the film. Nevertheless, in this original—and far more loquacious—version of *Days of Heaven*, the film loses much of its mystery and its weird and horrific elements along with it).

All Work and No Play

In their brutal yet beautiful landscapes, both *Badlands* and *Days of Heaven* offer a strange window into the soul of the country, "the old, weird America"[5] as it were. Whether we're following Kit and Holly as they walk down a small-town street or cruise across the plains in their Mercury Coupe or observe Abby and Bill toiling away in the wheat fields, these are familiar places. In fact, this is the quintessential American West. The purview of John Wayne, of frontiersmen, of the rugged individualism that allegedly defines the country. Yet through Malick's keen perspective, there's no sentimentality, no eager nostalgia. Instead, this is an unvarnished United States, one that's rotting away from the inside out. There's a dreamlike quality to the settings to be sure, but the gorgeous landscapes are forever threatening to devolve at any moment into the nightmarish.

More than that, the nightmare that's ready to erupt is hardly anything surreal in the vein of David Lynch. Malick's horrors are far more mundane than that. They're filled with everyday terrors, even pedestrian ones. In *Days of Heaven*, there are long, uninterrupted shots of workers in filthy mills and in filthy fields, of flames burning bright as hellfire in blast furnaces in Chicago, and of threshers slicing and dicing wheat (and whatever small animals get in the way) in Texas. In *Badlands*, we see garbagemen thanklessly

---

[3] Martin. "*Days of Heaven*: On Earth as It Is In Heaven"
[4] Malick. *Days of Heaven*.
[5] Ventura. "*Days of Heaven*."

collecting the detritus of a small town and cowboys capturing livestock and brutally force-feeding them pills. At one point during a grueling afternoon on a farm, Kit stands on the carcass of a cow, its jaw slung open, its black eyes wide, the reasons for its death unknown.

It's rare in the world of cinema to find films so razor-focused on hard labor and all the everyday misery that goes with it. It's a subtle but unmistakable subversion of the so-called American dream. As a culture, we venerate hard work in the abstract, blithely forgetting how grueling and backbreaking traditional blue collar labor truly is. Malick's films, especially *Badlands* and *Days of Heaven*, never shy away from the realities of perilous employment, how soul-crushing it can be to simply make an "honest" day's wage. And the truth is there are few things brimming with more existential horror than being indebted to an overlord who disregards your basic existence. For all his frailty and innocence, the Farmer is still the proverbial "Man," forcing the exhausted workers to spend their nights in the fields and small shacks, while he lives in relative luxury in a mansion of his own only yards away.

Days of Heaven notably opens in the grimy steel mills of Chicago where in a fit of impulsive rage, Bill inadvertently kills his foreman, setting into motion his flight from Illinois to Texas, with Abby and Linda in tow. In Malick's films, death and work are inextricably linked, one ultimately leading to the other, like a doomed snake devouring its own tale. Furthermore, the so-called days of heaven from the title arguably refer to the short-lived weeks in which Bill, Abby, and Linda coexist with the Farmer in relative ease after his wedding to Abby, the four of them swimming together in the lake, playing baseball in the fields, and dining in a pristine white gazebo overlooking the land. There's no wheat to tend, no obligations to meet. In Malick's vision, the closest you can get to bliss is a life that's far from the heavy toils of labor. Everything else is merely a routine horror in the making.

In the Embrace of the Cold, Unfeeling Universe
There's a deep level of emotional detachment in *Badlands* and *Days of Heaven*, something that's come to define the legacies of both films. Sissy Spacek's almost somnambulant voiceover as Holly gives the impression she's merely relaying the weather or some other prosaic news, rather than recounting a crime spree that remains notorious to this day.

In this detachment, there's a vein of cosmic horror, albeit one without a trace of elder gods. Instead, the unspeakable horror exists in the emotionless faces of Kit and Holly, two so-called lovers who are utterly lacking anything resembling love. Together, they're responsible for a brutal string of murders, but never for a moment do either of them seem to derive a bit of joy or exhilaration from it.

Even sex holds no pleasure for the two of them. "Is that all there is to it?" Holly asks after she and Kit consummate their relationship. "Gosh, what was everybody talking about?" Malick's is a universe imbued with unspeakable beauty but is wholly unfeeling. There's a pointlessness to it all. While other killers-on-the run films like *Natural Born Killers* have been accused of inspiring real-life crime sprees, it would be hard to imagine anyone watching *Badlands* and wanting to emulate its passive nihilism. There are no heroes here, no antiheroes either. It's a wasteland, devoid of feeling and—perhaps just as importantly—devoid of encouragement. If anything, it might be one of the most anti-crime films ever made, simply for how incredibly trite it makes murder look. In its casual detachment, *Badlands* seems to suggest that you can commit the ultimate sin, but you'll get nothing out of it. Homicide is merely more of the same.

There's also a sense of cosmic dread in the climax of *Days of Heaven*, as a literal plague of locusts descends on the property at precisely the same time the Farmer realizes he's been betrayed. It's as if Abby and Bill's cruel ruse has upset the balance of nature itself, sending all their lives spiraling into irrevocable heartbreak and chaos. But even still, there's an indifference to it. The locusts arrive, but they don't concern themselves with the people there or the lives and the land they're ruining. Their nature is to devour everything in their path, and that's precisely what they do, leaving no farm and no hope in their wake.

Exploring the Unlikely Gothic
The Gothic is alive and well in Malick's first two films, and that's particularly true of their use of young, female narrators. In *Days of Heaven*, Linda provides a shrewd voiceover that's at turns tragic, terrifying, and even hilariously macabre. Throughout it all, death is second nature to her, something omnipresent and inescapable. She speaks of the devil as though she knows him personally, like he's just another hitcher on the railroad or a worker

beside her in the field. "I think the devil was on the farm," she says, as we move ever closer to the inevitable blowout between the Farmer and Bill.

Linda's narration shares a certain precocious quality with that of Merricat Blackwood in Shirley Jackson's *We Have Always Lived in the Castle*—at once wise beyond her years and impossibly young. Merricat and Linda each see the world in terms of its inherent dangers. Both girls also reside on ancestral properties that will ultimately endure a reckoning of fire.

Similarly, Holly's narration in *Badlands* also has a decidedly Shirley Jackson quality to it: one of casual mistrust in others and the world at large. Like Merricat, Holly takes part in murder, if only as a bystander, and also like Merricat, she seems curiously unaffected by its consequences. Life and death don't seem to hold the same weight for them.

In keeping with the Gothic tradition, *Badlands* and *Days of Heaven* both feature life-altering fires on which the plots ultimately hinge. After Kit murders Holly's father, the first of many homicides in the film, he returns at night, douses the place in gasoline, and sets it alight. As the bright butter-yellow home—which already resembles a dollhouse—burns to the ground, the audience sees a literal dollhouse in Holly's bedroom as it turns to cinders as well. It's virtually undeniable: this moment marks the irrevocable end of Holly's innocence, a sort of threshold crossing from which there will be no return.

In *Days of Heaven*, fire marks the end of The Farmer's innocence as well. After weeks of speculation, he's at last seen Abby, the woman he refers to as an angel earlier in the film, for who she really is: a "con artist" as his foreman and old friend calls her. As the plague of locusts sweeps over the farm, he hopes that burning them out will save the wheat, all to no avail. Now with his one chance to find love gone forever and his farm likely lost as well, the Farmer tracks down Bill, intent on murdering him for his betrayal. But unlike Bill and Kit, he can't quite bring himself to commit such a vicious act. It's in the Farmer's single moment of hesitation that Bill gains the upper hand and fatally stabs him. After all, murder is not new territory for Bill, and old instincts die hard.

Once again, Bill must go on the run with Abby and Linda, this time taking an impromptu boat ride down the river that echoes Charles Laughton's seminal *The Night of the Hunter*[6]. But even as they manage to navigate past many unfriendly faces on the shore—people that Linda speculates are

---

[6] Ventura. "*Days of Heaven.*"

"calling for help or something, or they were trying to bury somebody"—the trio don't make it far before the authorities catch up with them, gunning Bill down in the water.

Likewise, Kit and Holly's journey does not end well for them. After a grim chase, they're both arrested, and Kit is taken away, presumably to face execution. While Malick's films frequently veer toward the unfeeling, they're also somewhere that killers don't ultimately go free. A small semblance of justice in a world that hardly seems to acknowledge such a thing exists.

Into an Uncertain Future
After the mixed reception of *Days of Heaven*, it would be twenty years before Malick made another film. His disappearance became one of the more legendary exits from cinema, a director leaving the industry at what should have been the top of his game.

Malick has, of course, resurfaced over the past quarter century, creating some of his most lauded works in the process, including *The Thin Red Line*, *The New World*, and *Tree of Life*. However, none of these films quite capture the same strange and indescribable energy of his first two cinematic outings. With *Badlands* and *Days of Heaven*, he effortlessly tapped into a vein of the Gothic, of the uncanny and the haunting, of the horrors shared every day by everyday people. These films are both breathtaking achievements, dripping with existential despair and exquisite beauty.

But for all their vast and wondrous landscapes, it's in the small moments of Malick's work where he shows just how awe-inspiring the world can be while also so casually cruel and dangerous. "Some sights that I saw was really spooky," Linda says in *Days of Heaven*, as she, Abby, and Bill are headed down the river together at night, fleeing her brother's latest murder. "It could be the dead coming for me."

Yet with menace and decay always looming in Malick's films, the dead aren't coming for us.

They're already here.

BIBLIOGRAPHY

Almendros, Néstor. "Photographing *Days of Heaven*." *American Cinematographer*. https://ascmag.com/articles/photographing-days-of-heaven.

Edward-Hopper.org. "*House by the Railroad*." https://www.edward-hopper.org/house-by-the-railroad.

Malick, Terrence. Original shooting script for *Days of Heaven*. http://www.dailyscript.com/scripts/daysofheaven.html.

Martin, Adrian. "*Days of Heaven*: On Earth as It Is in Heaven." *The Criterion Collection.* https://www.criterion.com/current/posts/555-days-of-heaven-on-earth-as-it-is-in-heaven.

Ventura, Elbert. "*Days of Heaven*." *Reverse Shot*. http://reverseshot.org/features/719/days-of-heaven.

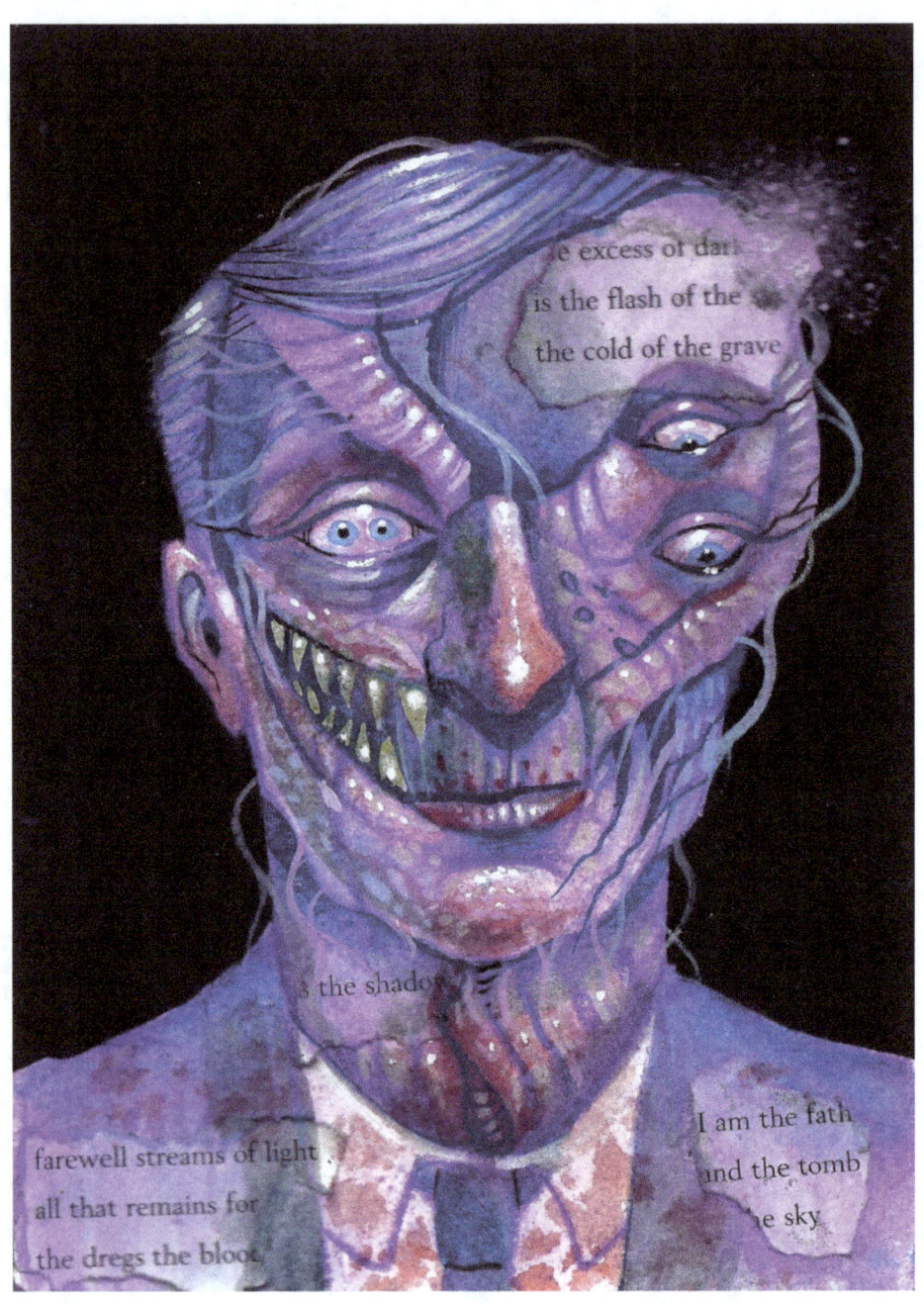

ART BY JASON BARNETT

Return to Office

Kristin Cleaveland

I WAS IN THE process of compiling a report when I heard the email notification. I clicked on the envelope icon. The subject line shouted, "RETURN TO OFFICE." Dread slipped down my spine and curled itself into my stomach.

I scrolled through the email, apprehension growing as I read.

"Dear Employee," it began. "We missed you! After much consideration, we at CompliChek Global have discontinued our remote work policy. Your presence is required at corporate headquarters 8:00 a.m. Monday. This arrangement is not open to negotiation. Upon arrival, please report to Room 001 to receive your new equipment. Thank you for your cooperation. See you soon!!"

I stared at the words on the screen, willing them to arrange themselves into any other configuration; one that meant I would not have to return to the building that had already claimed so much of my existence. But the words stayed the same, and when I closed my eyes to blot them out, the screen of the monitor glowed red against my eyelids.

It had been over a year since my employer had, by state order, allowed us to gather our laptops and plants, collect our reusable water bottles and stained coffee mugs, and leave the building to work from home. At the time, even through the fear and uncertainty of world events, I felt a thrill in my chest at the prospect of never returning to my squalid cubicle in that damp, leaky office. I could leave the smell of mildew and recirculated air behind, never more to hear the drone of fluorescent lights as I strained my eyes to read the figures in a column.

I worked as an analyst for CompliChek Global, a massive firm that conducted corporate audits to ensure that employees were in compliance with every dictate of company policy, no matter how picayune. I often felt remorse as I scrutinized spreadsheets and created reports, condemning nameless, faceless employees to disciplinary action or worse. Each day I was ensnared in a morass of red tape, a Byzantine labyrinth of bureaucracy. But my attempts at securing a different employer had as yet amounted to nothing.

I had long suffered from periods of intense anxiety and felt immense relief when the corporate office had announced that we would not be required to return to the office. Now, upon receiving the latest email, I felt my shoulders slump and the beginning of a migraine percolating around my temples.

I closed my company-issued laptop and stood up from my desk, even though it was still early in the afternoon. I knew my chat icon would show "away," which might prompt a confrontation with my manager, but I couldn't face another spreadsheet. I looked around my apartment, which, though small, had become a kind of sanctuary. The light was natural; my coffee pot was close at hand; I even had a small aquarium bubbling in the corner. The thought of leaving it for my tiny cubicle and the broken desk chair with a squeaky wheel left me with a sick feeling. I sat down on my couch and didn't move for hours.

That weekend, I spent most of my free time preparing for the dreaded return. From the clothes I had pushed to the back of my closet, I selected a white shirt, black dress pants, and a dark tie. When I started at CompliChek I had worn colorful ties, even one with a small fish pattern, but quickly realized that standing out from the crowd was frowned upon. I washed and ironed the clothes, then polished the pair of uncomfortable dress shoes I had hoped never to wear again.

I went to the store on the corner and purchased small items for packed lunches: bread, cold cuts, a few apples. Frozen pizzas because I knew that the evenings of being too tired to cook would return. A box of granola bars for my desk. The fluorescent lights of the grocery store portended the lighting in the office, which was somehow simultaneously too harsh and too dim.

On Sunday night, I laid awake for a long time. I tried a white noise app, melatonin, milk. I tossed and turned, then dreamed of wandering endless mazes. Every turn led to a dead end. And then, at 6:00 a.m., my alarm rang.

My morning routine felt both familiar and alien. There was a dull ache in my chest as I merged onto the freeway for my hour-long commute. When the inevitable traffic jam occurred, I looked around at the other drivers. They all wore the same dead-eyed look I knew was on my face.

Eventually, I pulled into the parking garage of my employer. I walked to the door and scanned my key card. A security guard stood in the lobby, directing employees to the elevator. There was a sign propped up on an easel beside him:

"Welcome back, CompliChek employees! Do NOT go to your desks! Proceed to Room 001."

I joined the line of dejected-looking coworkers, none of whom greeted each other with any enthusiasm. Our faces were unfamiliar to one another after years spent sequestered in cubicles. When an elevator arrived, we all squeezed in. I felt the crush of human bodies around me with a shock of anxiety; it had been so long. A man in front pushed the button labeled "B." We descended.

When the doors opened, I let out a breath I hadn't realized I was holding. The lighting in the basement gave the faces of my coworkers a sickly greenish cast. To our immediate left, we saw Room 001.

It had clearly served as a large storage room, but everything had been removed except for a long table with a stack of boxes behind it. Folding chairs were arranged facing the table. An easel stood before the table holding a poster that read:

"Put the 'I-CHEK' in "CompliChek!"

The poster also featured a picture of an employee with a rictus grin, giving the thumbs-up sign. The model for the poster wore what looked to be a pair of large safety goggles, held in place by a band that wrapped around the back of her head. Her eyes were wide and staring.

We made our way to the chairs and sat down. The unease I had felt for days was bubbling under my skin. My blood felt hot and close to the surface, my throat dry. I had forgotten my water bottle in the dishwasher at home.

From behind the stack of boxes, a woman stepped out. She was middle-aged, blonde, and dressed in a black skirt, white button-down shirt, and heels. Her lips were stretched in a wide smile.

"Welcome back, CompliChek employees!" she said, beaming enthusiastically. "We missed you so much!"

My coworkers and I looked around at each other. I could tell by the expressions on their faces that none of us had encountered this woman before.

"Thank you for coming to our first orientation session!" she continued. "We will be holding sessions for returning employees throughout the day.

You were all lucky enough to be selected first!" She paused here, as if waiting for us to express excitement. No one responded.

Undaunted, the blonde woman continued. "My name is Ashley Nelson, and I am the new Director of Human Resources for CompliChek Global! I am so excited to be embarking on this exciting adventure with all of you."

Someone in the back raised his hand. "How long is this going to take? I need to put my lunch in the fridge."

A brief flicker of annoyance flashed across Ashley's face, but her smile stayed intact. "I'm glad you are so eager to get started!" she replied.

The low drone of the lights was already worming its way into my brain. I shifted in the hard metal chair and loosened my tie as much as I thought I could get away with. The damp basement air felt stagnant as I breathed it in, trying to relax.

Another employee raised her hand. "Why did we have to come back, anyway? We were told we could work from home."

Ashley's eyes somehow grew even wider, giving her a fish-like expression. "Thank you so much for asking!" she exclaimed. "Let's get right to it." She looked out over the crowd. "As I'm sure you all know, recent events have put quite a strain on CompliChek Global. And, I'm sure," she said, her voice falling to a hushed tone, "on all of you. Some of you have even lost loved ones, and you have our sincere condolences." She paused for what she must have assumed to be an appropriate amount of reverence.

She continued, "That's why, here at CompliChek, we are eager to put all that unpleasantness behind us and embark on a new journey! We have called you back to the office because we want you to participate in our most exciting and ambitious rollout ever. This new technology we've created will change the face of compliance auditing permanently. And YOU get to be part of it!"

The sound of the lights seemed to be growing louder. I heard a dull roar as the air conditioning system kicked on. Even still, I had begun sweating. I unbuttoned the cuffs of my shirt and rolled my sleeves up to the elbows. My chest felt tight, and my breaths were shallow. I wiped my hands on my pants.

Ashley walked to the stack of cardboard boxes and pulled something out of the one on top. "I'd like to introduce to you CompliChek Global's latest innovation: the I-CHEK!" She held it up like a trophy in front of the gathered employees.

It was the device from the poster. A pair of goggles was attached to what appeared to be a metal band. "Let me show you how it works!" she exclaimed, her intonation climbing ever higher. She undid a clasp on the side and the band opened; she put the goggles over her eyes and clasped the band again. Behind the goggles, her eyes looked even larger than before. Her grin got even wider.

I rubbed my temples. Employees were mumbling to each other. I felt the familiar tingles of panic prickling at the edges of my brain; a cold chill spread through my body. The nerves in my feet began to tingle. I tried to breathe normally but could not.

Ashley was speaking faster now, her words pressured and unnatural. "The I-CHEK smart device is the absolute latest in compliance technology! It tracks the user's eye movements to ensure that he or she is directly focused on assigned tasks at all times. If the eyes stray too often—away from a computer monitor, for example—a report will immediately be compiled and sent to his or her supervisor via the I-CHEK app!"

None of the employees were talking now. We all stared, transfixed.

Ashley continued: "I'm sure that you understand that now, after recent events, employee monitoring is more important than ever! Business owners have been hit so hard lately, and they need to make sure they are maximizing their employees' full potential. After all, employees are a corporation's most valuable asset!

"That's why the I-CHEK device not only tracks employee eye movements to ensure productivity, but it also has the ability to produce alerts that keep employees on task! If an employee's focus is interrupted for too long, the metal band will vibrate, providing a gentle reminder to get back to the task at hand. If ignored, the vibrations will get gradually more intense—but we know you will all be responsive immediately!"

I felt faint. The man next to me stood up. "This is bullshit," he said. "I quit." He threw his ID badge onto the metal folding chair and headed for the large double doors of Room 001.

Ashley spoke in a smoothly threatening voice. "I'm so sorry you feel that way," she said. "However, I would like to remind you that if you quit, you will not be eligible to receive unemployment. This could also mean losing your healthcare coverage, which we know now is more important than ever."

The man stopped. He didn't turn around, but his shoulders slumped forward.

"Also, CompliChek is currently in *very* exciting talks with many other leaders in the compliance audit community! Many are looking into implementing the I-CHEK device in their own offices. Soon, I-CHEK will be the standard throughout the industry. It will be very difficult to find an employer if you aren't willing to embrace the new technology." For just a moment, her voice lost its perky inflection. "I think we had all better just get used to it."

The man turned around, defeated, and trudged back to his seat. I saw the way he clenched his jaw and knew he would soon have a headache like mine. No one else said a word.

Ashley went on to explain that, in addition to the "gentle vibrations," the device could also admit a high-frequency noise that would offer employers another option for an "attention reset." There was yet another feature—one that was still under development—that could provide "the *very* mildest of electric shocks for full focus potential."

"The I-CHEK is actually very helpful for employees!" Ashley said. She must have noted the looks of horror on our faces. "I've been using mine for a few weeks now, and I am so much more productive! It's great for your wellness, too. Once you have accrued a certain amount of eye strain, it reminds you to take a break of up to three minutes!"

My jaw was clenched tight enough to break my teeth. No one said a word as Ashley began calling us forward, one by one, to receive our I-CHEK devices. After everything we had experienced over a year, the culture shock of returning to the office and being faced with this absurdity had stunned us all into silence.

When it was my turn, I felt unsteady on my feet. My surroundings took on a haze of unreality, augmented by the disorientation of being in public at all. I rested my palm on the table in the front for support.

Ashley took an I-CHEK out of the box. "This will feel a little strange at first, but trust me, after a few days you won't even know it's there! It doesn't bother me at all anymore!" Her eyes didn't meet mine but looked into the distance over my shoulder. I hadn't been this near to anyone in over a year. As she leaned in to fit the device to my face, I saw beads of sweat on her brow. Her thick makeup had settled into the fine lines of her face. The perfume she wore was strong, but I also noticed a thin, astringent scent radiating from her. I knew from experience that it was fear.

As she tightened the band around my forehead, my migraine flared. I must have winced because she loosened it just a little. "You'll get used to it," she said softly, just to me. I heard the resignation in her voice and knew that there was no way out.

Ashley raised her voice and addressed the group. "When you have received your I-CHEK device, you may proceed upstairs to your desk! You have all been reassigned to the third floor. You will be pleasantly surprised to see that the cubicles have been removed! We have a new arrangement we call the Accountability Pod. I'm sure you'll love it!"

Trying to stave off a full-blown panic attack, I stopped in the restroom next to the elevator. My hands were shaking as I ran the cold water in the sink. I tugged at the metal band of the I-CHEK, trying to remove it so I could splash my face. It would not come loose. Another employee stepped out of a bathroom stall and saw me. He shook his head.

"It won't come off," he said. "I heard someone from accounting saying they're on some kind of timer. They'll release automatically at 5 p.m. Otherwise, you need a supervisor's permission."

The goggles of his I-CHEK were fogged from the inside, and I realized he must have been crying in the stall. "My wife got sick," he said, as if by way of explanation. "I really need this job."

Not knowing how to respond, I extended my hand. He hesitated for a moment, then grasped it tightly. Though I had initiated it, the contact came as a shock; I hadn't shaken a hand in over a year.

As he washed his hands, I made my way out of the restroom and to the elevator. I pressed the button for the third floor.

When the elevator doors opened, I suddenly realized what Ashley had meant by "Accountability Pod." All the desks had been arranged in a circle, with no cubicle walls between them. In the center of this panopticon was what I assumed to be a supervisor's desk, which was shaped like a semi-circle, enabling its occupant to turn his or her chair in a complete circle. I approached the fishbowl arrangement of desks with dread.

A man sat at the middle desk. Several coworkers were already situated at the surrounding workstations. "Welcome!" he said, then asked for my name and pointed to one of the desks. "This is you!" he announced brightly.

I drew back the desk chair and sat down. After a moment, I realized that the chair was in a fixed position; I would not be able to rotate or lean back. I slowly unpacked my work bag: my company laptop, my bagged lunch, the box of granola bars. More coworkers gradually arrived and took their seats. When all the desks were occupied, the supervisor stood from his chair. "Welcome back, CompliChek employees! We missed you so much!" he began, in the same tone of forced gaiety Ashley Nelson had employed. "My name is David O'Neill, and I will be your temporary supervisor. At some point in the near future, I will be reassigned and one of you will take over my position! The role, which comes with a slight increase in pay, will go to the employee who has demonstrated the most dedication to establishing compliance." He paused and looked around the circle, waiting for us to absorb his exciting news.

No one replied. David continued, "The new, mutually beneficial workplace arrangement will allow us all to keep one another accountable! If you see a coworker displaying noncompliant behavior, give that person a gentle reminder to refocus. You'll be doing that person a favor by contributing to team productivity. If you see the noncompliant behavior continue, please reach out to me, and I will take further action."

We all stared down at our desks. The metal band of the I-CHEK was tight around my skull.

"Of course, the I-CHEK will remind us, too! This is truly a cutting-edge productivity tool. But just in case, *I* will *check* on you, too!" He chuckled, looking proud of himself. One or two employees made sounds of forced amusement.

I opened my laptop and stared at my screen. My eyes already felt dry and scratchy. I brought up a spreadsheet and tried to absorb the data it contained. As the minutes wore on, I heard employees around me let out various small gasps and murmurs. I could only assume that their focus reminders had been activated.

At around 10:00 a.m., my stomach growled. I turned to reach for the granola bars on my desk. A sharp buzz sent a chill down my spine.

I saw David get up from his desk, looking down at his phone. He walked over to my workstation. "Hi! According to the I-CHEK app, you have not yet accrued enough eye strokes for the allotted three-minute break. Your eyes are still capable of a high level of productivity, so that's great! You will be alerted when it's time for a rest."

I was too stunned to reply. Focusing my eyes directly on my laptop screen, I set the granola bars back down on the desk. "That's the spirit!" David said. He walked back to his desk.

The day proceeded in this fashion, with a short break for lunch, until I was startled by the sensation of the I-CHEK band loosening. "Congratulations on a great day of productivity!" David exclaimed. It was 5:00 p.m. precisely. "Please turn your I-CHEK devices in for safekeeping. The technology is proprietary, so the devices must remain in the building until further notice. They will be reassigned to you at 8:00 a.m. tomorrow. Have a great night!"

I drove home as if in a fog, my mind unable to fully process the day's events. I sat in silence without even the radio, staring straight ahead. I was afraid to avert my eyes for even a second. I could still feel the phantom sensation of the I-CHEK on my head.

When I arrived home, I untied my dress shoes and left them on the mat. I fed my fish, then preheated the oven for a frozen pizza. I removed my tie and sank onto the couch. I thought about my options. I could not simply quit my job; I had student loan debt, a car loan, and rent to pay. My savings were minimal, as my employer's salaries were not generous. I took out my phone and opened a job-hunting app. I typed "compliance analyst" into the search box.

Several local results were returned. I clicked on the first listing and reviewed the qualifications. At first the job looked promising: I had a bachelor's degree, relevant work experience, and the skills the employer was looking for. As I scrolled down the page, an item at the bottom of the listing caught my eye:

"I-CHEK compliance required."

A cold chill spread down my spine and throughout my extremities. My breaths became shallow and quick. I returned to the original list of search results and scrolled through them all. Every single one was the same.

The oven pinged loudly, signaling that it was preheated. I remained on the couch. Outside the window, the sun sank into the clouds, sending long shadows across the room. I could hear the bubbling of the aquarium. I stared straight ahead as darkness fell.

ART BY VISHNU SHYAMALA PRASAD

The Case Against the Dream

Armel Dagorn

A TRAIN DRIVER KNOWS, of course, their line's schedule, the exact instant their train must make it into such and such station, as if an in-built clockwork moved them. So maybe it wasn't so strange that I came to know with such certitude, like a rumble in my blood, the time I got to the bridge. Sometimes I thought this hellish regularity had nothing to do with me though, with my pushing the levers, flicking switches, but that I was simply a pawn slotted into a great, well-oiled machine that comprised every turning gear of the train, the singing of the rail.

I told Old Bellec about the sinking feeling in my gut that never failed to appear at a specific point, some fifty meters before the bridge. He sat in the jump seat, after coming into the cab to say hi.

"What's it like, this feeling?"

"Like, something shifting."

I took my eyes off the tracks. Old Bellec was the only colleague I'd ever told about doubting my fitness for the job. I guess I liked him from the start, as he was one of the few who didn't make coarse jokes in my presence.

"Or is it like a gear not catching?"

I tried to picture it and nodded hesitantly. Bellec's lips relaxed into a smile.

"Or maybe you're just going nuts," he added, "or I am."

I laughed. I'd started talking to him a few months into the job, when I was moved to the night shift, and the dream started visiting me. I'd even told him about my childhood, how I'd got my love of trains from my grandfather. I drove the train at night, then went home to closed shutters, and despite the little light that filtered through whatever sleep I got, I dreamed of night. Then I woke up, and took a shift after a fitful sleep, and felt the grip of its horrors on me until I reached the final stop.

"Don't worry," Old Bellec told me. "Everyone gets it. To a man—or woman. Goes with the job. The toll it takes, I guess."

In the dream I found myself driving, pulling the same levers I did at work, checking the same panels. After a while, the shadows around, the vague moving silhouettes of trees and power lines dispersed, and the train followed the tracks into the sky, and shortly something appeared. I slammed on the brakes, and the shape shifted, turned toward the train, toward me, faced me, tried to resolve itself into something human. I pushed the brake, but nothing happened, and I crashed awake in my bed. Often, I still had a couple of hours before my alarm was set, but I'd turn it off and get up anyway, wobble to the shower, try to rinse off the stench of terror. I was afraid to go back to sleep, that again I wouldn't be able to stop, and I feared if it happened just once more, I wouldn't be able to go to work then, step on my train and turn its awesome mass into motion.

"Can't I make it stop?"

"The train, do you mean? Or the dream? You won't have much luck with the train, I'd say," Bellec said. "Brakes are faulty. It's like you jumped off a plane without a parachute. It might be dream logic, but it's still logic. Might be able to work on the dream, though."

"How?"

I glanced at Bellec. He sat pensive, his eyelids nearly closed, and in the minute rocking of the train, I thought he might have fallen asleep.

"You have to find out why you're crashing."

"What?"

Old Bellec raised his chin from his chest and sighed.

"Look, everyone has their thing. Some of the guys think of beaches, of mountain summits, or bouncy castles before they go to sleep. Anything to force their minds off the tracks that lead wherever they don't want to go. I've seen some still sitting in their cab, at their final stop, when they should have been on their way home, pushing the brakes again and again, building an empirical case against the dream that would have as much value in the phantom realm as old francs in this here shop," he said, pointing out the window, without looking, to a lonely little shop at a crossroads.

"Look, you might think I'm crazy, but I think that there's a reason you dream you're running someone over. It's not innocent—maybe *we* are not innocent. There's something at the root of it, and you should try to find out what it is. What's there at the heart of it, at the beginning."

Old Bellec's eyelids drooped again, as if he hadn't been addressing me but the air.

"And that would make it stop?"

"I don't know," he said, glancing at me. "But it would be something." He looked at the door then and rose slowly. We were arriving at Kerhuon, and even though he hadn't once looked out the window the whole time he'd been in the cab, he must have felt each rail, each bolt in his bones, and known exactly where we were.

The root of it. I'd never thought driving trains would become the source of such anxiety. The running over, the crashing into things, the derailings—none of this had ever crossed my mind. Neither had I imagined the boring, repetitive routine my colleagues often complained about. All through training, and for months after I started on the job, a childish excitement came over me when I got on and sat in the cab. Like I'd been allowed something I shouldn't have.

As a child, I'd spent most school holidays at my grandfather's. The logistics of it are unclear now—how and what did he feed me, how did we spend those weeks, the two of us? My grandmother had died when I was very young, and I had no recollection of her, only vague memories of pictures blown into a ghostly character by fragments of stories. The time I remember was spent up in the attic. He had built a gigantic model train in there, a looping scenery that stretched from wall to wall. I guess after losing his wife he'd thrown himself into that hobby, but it was hard to imagine he hadn't always been painting little cows, crafting bridges and fixing the station master's house.

A trapdoor led to the attic and took us right to the middle of the landscape. We stood there, the two of us like giants rising out of some hell-bound sink-hole, surveying the land and nitpicking at the angles trees sprang out, the nearness of taxis to the station, the gentleness of hillocks. From there, all the perspectives worked, and the rows of model houses blended seamlessly into the trompe l'oeil ones painted onto the landscape, blurring the line between what was real and what wasn't.

Granddad had a small worktable he pulled from under the land, and when things needed mending farther afield, we crawled under the surface, where between trestles gaps had been left in the mounts of boxes of tools and materials. We navigated the burrows, trying not to bump our heads and fell a wood overground, or slay a herd, shake a hamlet loose on its foundations. We emerged at the edges of the room, where other holes punctured the landscape, and from where the scenery took strange slants.

There we found more tools, scissors, glue and paint tubes, left stuck in the cross section between the earth crust and the tabletop, archaeological proof of some divine tinkerer. On the walls, postcards and pictures were thumb-tacked, rail-crossed hollows and quaint cottages, stations of various yesteryears with men in top hats and ladies with parasols, more modern pictures of high-speed trains.

I often wondered what Granddad was after, if all those prompts were to help him recreate a real place, or if, like a mad scientist, he was trying to design, from parts, a utopia, give life to a tiny, perfect patch of land.

Whichever it was, I remember the sensation of peace, standing in the middle of this papier-mâché world, watching the train circle the land in its inhuman regularity. Granddad didn't let me control the train, always said I was too young, and the power he had, his hand on the throttle, impressed me. As if rather than a tiny toy train it was the world itself he coaxed into its revolutions. I couldn't say how many hours, days, I spent staring at the train as he sat hunched over figurines, mumbling to himself.

He liked to give the characters that populated the land backstories, and he'd have the shopkeeper wear black eternally for the loss of his mother or curse the old mad one on the platform bench who wouldn't stop telling commuters fables.

"You useless twat!" he'd say, painting clothes onto a running character.

The Case Against the Dream

"You think the train will wait for you?"

He could be grumpy, but he mostly vented his foul moods on blank little plastic figurines, and what I remember of him still now is the benevolent power, the life he put in motion. And in truth in later life, in pursuing the career born in that attic, I tried to regain this sense of moving great things for the good of others.

"Did you ever find it?" Old Bellec asked me when I told him about these childish notions. By then I felt like the dreams had started to seep into my waking days. The previous evening, a few kilometers out of Pleyber-Christ, I'd run into a majestic buck. It had stood there on the tracks, head high, looking straight at me. The buffer hit its flank in a dull thud, and even though at 280kph I shouldn't have been able to distinguish all these sounds, I made out the dry crack of its antlers, the splintering ribs and squish of crushed organs. One sound after the other, in a meticulously composed symphony of death. A guy from the cleaning crew later told me they only found an antler, and gooey bits of fur. There'd been a tear in the high fence on either side, like a furious monster had refused to see its forest cut in two.

I got off the train in Pleyber-Christ, shaking, and that's what had made me tell Bellec about these old yearnings. As if talking about it could get me back there, to that simpler consciousness.

I looked at him, at the old creases in his face, and snorted.

"I guess kids have an oversimple vision of things," I said.

"Yeah. The whole thing's not quite a merry-go-round, is it?"

I'd heard the stories—Old Bellec had been a driver until recently. One day, with only a few years to go until retirement, he'd filled in the paperwork to apply for a position as ticket inspector. He'd taken a pay cut, of course, but passed the entrance test easily, after all these years of service, without once opening the rulebook. I never asked him his age, but people said he could have retired years ago—should have—but that he just couldn't leave, that if he did his whole world would just derail.

"Is this," Bellec asked, "the root of it? This great sense of peace? Is this really what you're looking for?"

"What do you mean?"

"You know sometimes, we don't remember well. We see the past as we want to see it. Hell, we see the present as we want to see it."

"I was very happy in that attic."

"Were you? Would you go back there? If you could?"

I thought of it. After my grandfather's death I hadn't once set foot in the house. I had sometimes in later years driven past it, seen the already old house show its age more each time. It hadn't sold for years, and when finally it did, it was for crumbs, and to someone who sat on it, wanted the plot for some future venture.

Every time I passed, years apart sometimes, I thought of the attic, the memory of it crumbling just like I imagined the real thing did, my grandfather's fantasy collapsing on itself from the pressure of the world around. Cobwebbed stations. Locomotives falling through the rotting cardboard land.

When I got home that morning, I went straight to my bedroom. On the top shelf of the wardrobe, at the back, accessible only by tiptoeing onto a chair and burrowing through paper bags filled with useless things, was an old shoebox I hadn't set eyes on in years. I knelt down by it on the floor, pulled off the thick elastic band that bound it. I hazily remembered its contents, a few objects blurred by the fogs of childhood.

I picked up the little locomotive first, felt its weightlessness, traced the embossed hull. How tiny. Inconsequential. Once, I'd said, after Granddad had told me for the hundredth time I was too young to control the train, that it didn't matter because when I grew up, I'd be a train driver. He'd snorted.

"No, you won't," he'd answered without looking at me. "It's not a girl's job." After a few minutes, when he noticed I was sulking, he said there were other jobs, in the dining car for instance.

I dropped the locomotive on the floor—it only made the smallest tock.

I examined the first postcard. I must have stared at it too the last time I'd opened this dusty time-capsule, as it lay on top of the pile. It was the bridge, in the washed-out tones of decades-old postcards, which of course added to the idyllic feel of the picture. The elegant arches of the stone viaduct crossed the picture from one woods-blanketed hill to the other, and on second look, you could spot the discreet mosaic of the town below. But, of course, what first caught one's attention was the train crossing the void, the boxy locomotive, the red carriages trailing behind. I recalled as a girl staring at the picture, hoping to find a passenger's face in the tiny squares of the windows, wondering what their features might express. I never found any, though, and neither did the locomotive show its driver. As if the train, and this setting, were just too pretty to be true.

From the driver's seat I never got this particular point of view, but it was unmistakably my bridge, the one I took my train over. The one that insisted on crossing the hollow of my sleep.

I guess the evidence of this postcard, and the many that had covered the attic walls, suggested Granddad must have been striving for some form of reality. Behind the card, his handwriting read: *Northern end—Watch out for disjunction*. In my anxious state, I took it for an instant as an injunction, a warning such as those that often came over the radio as I was driving or as must have been passed on to my colleagues coming through after I'd run over that buck.

When I managed to escape the nonsensical twists of my mind, I told myself that it had to have been Granddad's instructions to himself, that in building a likeness of the postcard's bridge he had come across difficulties and written down a reminder of the adjustments needed. I conjured the attic of my memory, its walls lined with postcards and pictures, and adjusted this image to the knowledge that every single one of them might have had notes on what was wrong with the world, what had to be feared, or fixed.

Why had Granddad sent it to me? There was an old stamp and the address of my parents, where we'd lived at the time. I couldn't remember these exchanges of ours, how we had shared this world no one else cared about. Had he sent it to me as homework? But I'd never done more than simple tasks for him. I usually just stood back and observed him paint a path here, fashion a hedge there, no matter how much I'd wanted to have a hand at it myself. Or was it to tell me that the problem remained? That it was one of this world's irreparable things, and that I would have to live with it, live carefully?

That night I went to bed serene, the only bridge on my mind a foot tall mishmash of sticks, glue, and faux-stone paper, the only risk that its end might come slightly undone from the papier-mâché hill.

Still, I came to within my sleep, my hand flat on the control board, more in shock to steady my dream self than to drive the train. The trees and fences, the odd shed and cows we passed reflected the moon's light. As I passed them at high speed, I was left wondering if what had just disappeared was maybe more, or less, than what I thought I'd seen. These ghostly forms, wind-shaken cypresses mimicking devils, troughs hunkering like tanks on the warpath, all seemed inhabited with more than the mere material they should have been. As if, once humans left, they let the fearsome object souls that governed them free.

I had a certain awareness, which I felt must mean things were changing, moving towards something, and I tried in my mind, my dream self's mind, to recall the postcard, its sepia daylight. But the land fell then, on either side of me, the trees disappeared, felled, and I found myself on the bridge, in silence, the silence of the train's permanent rumble suddenly unburdened by echo. Below, the town was dark, its inhabitants dark, dreaming a wondrous metal snake across the coal sky.

Then I crashed into light.

"Maybe this isn't the start, then." Old Bellec said when I told him I'd had the dream again. "The attic. Maybe the problem isn't the bridge. *Watch out for disjunction*—maybe—maybe something is out of place."

This is when Bellec made me ride the train. Any time I had off, I boarded my own line. Sometimes Bellec was on duty, but if he wasn't, he rode with me. He made me walk down the aisles, sit down next to regular passengers and chat with them, play-act that I was just another carefree traveler and not a tormented driver who feared she was rushing hundreds into violent death. I sat in the dining car and had a glass of wine and looked out the window as the train cleared the fields and dived into the near-void of the bridge. Every time, at every passage, a little hand pinched my heart, but the true test was at night.

All of Old Bellec's exercises were for nothing. I started feeling foolish—

maybe I shouldn't have confided in him. He'd managed to make me tell him things I'd never told anyone else.

How I saw Granddad die.

He'd been showing me the little figurine of me, the one I'd badgered him to make until he'd painted my haircut and favorite jumper onto one of his blank characters.

"Put me in the locomotive!" I'd said.

Granddad grimaced. I knew he didn't like his little world disrupted, but it meant a lot to me.

"Please, Granddad!"

"You think you can be whatever you want?" he burst out. "I made you, isn't that enough? Always more, isn't it?"

He slammed me down then, my little figurine, on the model, and I was so focused on it, bothered by seeing it there, standing on the tracks, when I could hear the train already rolling back around this side of the room, that it took me a couple of seconds to notice Granddad's face had gone red, clenched. He brought his hand to his chest before collapsing to the ground, ripping a ravine in the cardboard land as he fell.

I thought Bellec's response to my terror, knowing all this, diminished it. I felt like he was just entertaining himself by playing the part of a psychiatrist— or what he thought a psychiatrist might be.

In fact, if I hadn't witnessed colleagues having heartfelt conversations with him, I might have suspected they were setting me up. Still, they looked at me then as if I were a little crazy. Every time I traveled on a day off, a colleague on the platform or the ticket inspector on board would nod hello, a little embarrassed. It was almost worse when it was guys I didn't know, as I had to show my employee card. Word later got back to me that it was known, beyond my immediate colleagues, that there was a mad one on the Paris-Brest line riding it on her days off.

So, I almost didn't go when Bellec told me I should visit Morlaix. I was working up the nerves to say that I wasn't going to go along with his crazy DIY therapy anymore when he told me that he'd taken a day off so he could accompany me on this strange pilgrimage to the terminus of my terror.

I nodded, and a couple of days later we got off the train in Rennes when our shifts ended. I focused on rushing passengers, their mundane to-and-fros, when the PA crackled on.

"Due to an incident on the tracks, train 5678 to Bordeaux will…"

I felt Bellec's hand on my shoulder. "Come on. Platform two." I think my eyes were closed as he towed me to the local train bound for Morlaix.

The best view I'd had of the town was from the postcard, its age-tainted jumble of old houses. When I passed it at night, I only got a glimpse of streetlights and windows, the square shapes of houses only guessed at. And in my dreams—the dark. It was strange to be down there, to see the shadow pit of my sleep as a quaint little touristy town. The narrow streets were bathed in sunlight, the timbered houses leaning towards each other in the stoop of old age.

I surprised myself by smiling at Old Bellec. I felt light. I wondered if his plan had been, in bringing me here, to simply take my mind off my worries by taking me sightseeing, rather than to continue the charade of therapy. Maybe this was what I needed. A reset. The previous week I'd driven in a fevered state, and at times there was a trembling at the edges of my vision, and chunks of land, whole fields disappeared, sunk in tremendous swallows, there where the eye sees lights better, but objects blurrier. I'd turn my head and find the fields intact, the meadows unbroken, but in that glance a shadow formed on the tracks, and the constant back and forth, the sensation of constantly missing a grave danger, exhausted me.

Here and there in our walks, we came across scenic views of the town and the bridge. We spotted the 3:42 to Quimper crossing the void, so small up there in the landscape. It wasn't quite the point of view of the postcard, and I didn't know if it would change anything.

We sat at a terrace for coffee, and when Old Bellec came back from buying cigarettes, he had a postcard in hand.

"Your bridge," he said. I glanced at it and saw it was the same postcard that lay buried in my wardrobe. This one was new—forty-years new. I imagined it sitting on its metal display, scorned by tourists for decades.

Bellec frowned and took out his thick glasses from his breast pocket.

"What?"

"Hum." He angled the postcard to the light, close to his face. He put it down on the table in front of me then, shrugging. I leaned over it. I couldn't see anything, except that it was in better condition than mine. He gave it a tap, on the line, ahead of the locomotive. I saw. Or at least, I think I did. A darker line, an upright shape. Something that could have been a tree trunk, a pole, a person. Or just the way a shadow fell on the hill.

That night, after a hearty meal in the hotel's restaurant, we took to our bedrooms early. They'd given us those connected rooms, and after we said good night opening each our door, I got ready for bed hearing Old Bellec do the same through the door, huffing from his old joints. I felt bad for him. No matter how silly or misguided it had been, he'd done a lot for me.

I woke up to "The brakes are working, the brakes are working," and sat up straight, heart racing. I could see a line of light under the door that separated my room from Bellec's, the shadow of his feet. "The brakes are working," I heard again, the voice reaching me through the wood. I sat there silent, listening to what could have been his heavy breathing or simply the background hum of the world. I don't know how long we stayed like this, but finally he walked away from the door, and I heard his body on the springs of the mattress.

The next day we didn't talk much as we filled our plates from the breakfast buffet and sat down to eat. He didn't mention his night intervention, and I thought he looked spent.

"I'll have to take the 9:20 back, love. Duty calls."

I told him I would take a later train, enjoy Morlaix a little more. I tried to look cheery. Bellec thought he had failed—I'd dreamed again.

When Old Bellec left, I told reception I'd be staying an extra night and set out for another day of idle roaming. For dinner, I ventured away from the safety of the hotel's restaurant. I ate in a tiny creperie in one of those cobbled streets that seemed only reachable by chance, by letting your brain idle and your feet roam. I felt at peace. I ate slowly, enjoying the break from the company of colleagues, from restaurant specials paid with vouchers.

The waiter came with an awkward look on his face and asked me if I would like anything else. I looked down at my empty dessert plate, the room empty except for one couple, standing up already, laying notes on the table. I thanked him and said I was okay, asked for the bill. I don't know how long I'd been staring into space, but in that time, lost in nothingness, I'd felt happier, lighter, than I had for as long as I could remember. More in my place.

Outside, the air was nicely sharp. I looked in the direction of the hotel, the street opening onto a larger one. I headed off the other way, along houses of crooked stone. Looking up, I couldn't see the bridge, but I felt it there over me, looming like a storm cloud in the night.

I meandered my way into a cul-de-sac and stopped where the asphalt did. The town itself stopped there, and before me the ground rose, steeply, into a scrawny forest. A trail of obviously beaten earth ventured up, and before I knew what I was doing I had entered the ominous silence of the undergrowth. The going was tough, and I had to grab saplings to haul myself up, but I never doubted the direction I had to follow. I felt as if drawn by some strange upwards gravity, reeled in by the moon's irresistible pull.

I came to the fence right where a picket sagged, the earth it stood on loosened, and passing on the other side was just a matter of pulling the top down and stepping over the chain-link.

A train driver always knows, of course, their line's schedule, and as I got on the gravel, over the rail, one foot in and one foot out, standing there over the singing metal, its thrum between my feet, I knew there shouldn't be a train. I looked to the bridge that a few steps away projected into darkness, and the light there grew from pinpoint to ball bearing to everything, and I felt, as it engulfed the night, right.

Psithurism

T. M. Morgan

This morning I found a leather braid bracelet outside the second bedroom. Just lying on the carpet, with the door closed tight behind it. A bronze snap clicks when I squeeze it. Snug around my wrist.

"Thank you," I whisper through the door.

The morning arrives, vague as always. Did I sleep? Coffee is already made when I wake. Brahms streams in every room. *Ein Deutsches Requiem, nach Worten der heiligen Schrift*. A German Requiem, To Words of the Holy Scriptures. I am not religious, do not in fact grasp what I am, if I am anything. The house simply knows I love this piece of music. A contraption announces bacon and eggs. It astounds me to not understand how all my provisions arrive.

The house loves me. I feel it. Like the bracelet. Such beauty in the craftsmanship, an intricate triplet weaving of strands that must symbolize trinity. Me, the house, and...?

The deck in back looks down the mountainside onto Greenbriar Lake. Its ripples flutter with sunlight. In the summer, such a view is impossible with the thick growth; the current fall provides the best of it, the desiccated leaves having mostly fallen. I breathe in. Close my eyes. An alarm sounds from inside. A reminder. For?

"Your medicine," the soft female voice says from the deck speaker.

Right. In the master bathroom, all my things are arranged on the right side of his and hers matching sinks. The *hers* side is barren. I remember thinking that clutter on the *her* side would be improper. One of those strange thoughts we get in our heads, an idea that appears to have no foundation yet becomes essential. "Keep your things to your side." The house wants me to believe I am leaving it pristine for the day someone arrives to use it. "Maybe," I told the house. My pills are dispensed from a small chute. One light blue pill, one pink, two bicolor red-and-white, and a tiny white, oval one. I've forgotten their names.

I swallow them with a palmful of water. Better. Already the tremors in my stomach ease. And the bracelet: pulsing with the urge to leave the house. The long upstairs hallway swirls like a funhouse mirror when I leave the master bedroom. The second bedroom door sits halfway down on the left; but all the way down on the right, the third bedroom waits. I turn away. For a time, I put yellow tape—like a crime scene—across the second door to remind myself—so often forgetful—to not enter. Even now my fists clench to think of it. My vision is hazy anyway. Beige carpet. A dome light that changes colors based on my mood. Doors painted blue. Count: one, two, three doors (one behind me). Count: eleven steps going to the first floor. A bad number. I deal with it.

A modern house built with the most impressive architectural design. Do I need to open doors? No. All automated, all foreseen by the house. But being here day after day: did the thing within grow after my arrival or simply reveal itself in slow steps? Much like love, it can be hard to remember when it came, when it turned from one thing into another.

I walk to the second bedroom door and open it, cautious, taking care not to put any part of my being inside. Within, a dark room; no light automatically turns on. I have to request it. The room is bare: four walls painted white, an unadorned window that looks out on trees, a many-crystaled chandelier. I close the door. Open it again. There are immeasurable stars and a galaxy spinning wildly. In the foreground, a reddish nebula spews gasses across the cosmos. The walls of the room are translucent like a glass box jutting into infinity.

Back in the bathroom, I wash my hands vigorously. I am kept from most germs while inside, but I feel them, nonetheless, crawling across me, burrowing. The hot water begins to burn, the soap like acid. But it's good. Such a day! The bathroom matches my mood: light blue tile interspersed with indigo diamonds. The counters are a meticulously tidy gray, while the cabinets below are white. Gold faucets and showerheads. Stand up shower with jacuzzi tub (which I've never used). And my reflection in the mirror, brooding with a foreign face. Is that me? I know it is, as no one else lives here. A round of white features topped with black hair. Prosopagnosia. Face blindness. Every morning I greet a stranger.

Downstairs I find that night has almost fallen. Another day passed with no recollection. I walked up, took my pills, stood in the hallway, and...? Did I enter the second bedroom? I think of the thing in the third bedroom...maybe monstrous is the appropriate word for what resides there. Did I speak with it? All that matters, really, is that it loves me profoundly, would never allow me to be hurt. So monstrous, as a word, seems unfair. Different. Unique. Those work better.

The lake looks magnificent from the deck. A small hut on the pier and lone security lamp above it offer bright pricks of light. The sky looks a mix of light orange against a backdrop of purple beyond the rolling mountaintop to the east. The heavens glitter in fractured lines across the surface of the water. The house wants me to go there.

"Okay," I say. "I'll go. It's a beautiful night anyway."

At the car, I look up. The moon is full, with a sliver of black cut away on its waxing side. A breeze blows, rustling the forest around me. I slide into the backseat.

"The marina," I say.

Her voice whispers from the speakers. "Some music on the way?"

"Berlioz. And drive slowly. I want to hear the wind."

The car backs out and goes through the many curves down the mountain. The car comes with the house. A package. I don't understand the technology, but all my needs are met. All my needs except for one.

We park. I rub absently at the leather bracelet on my left wrist. I often come here. Greenbriar Lake is, in fact, my only destination. Never beyond the limits of the town of Greenbriar. When here, I count the canoes, which are rented by the hour most of the year. There are twelve in rotation. Often, I will count the number still docked, subtract one number from the other, and determine how many canoes are on the lake.

I sit with the window down for a long time. Warm for this late in the year. Frogs croak; cicadas buzz with their raspy song; crickets add melodic vibrations so that all the sounds create a see-saw rhythm between them. The lake reflects the moon and the billions of stars. Only minor ripples roll across the surface, just enough to give the reflections an impressionistic appearance.

I see one of the canoes floating freely. Too dark to make out its green exterior, I instead see the silhouette. "Door," I say, and there is a click followed by the rear driver's door swinging out. A thin sidewalk circles the body of water along its full perimeter, though in some areas sidewalk turns into boardwalk as it crosses over pockets of marshland. Here at the marina and parking lot, a strip of sandy shore offers access to a swimming area. I cross to the water's edge. The boat floats only ten feet from shore.

"Hey!" It is a woman's voice. "What are you doing?"

"I saw this canoe floating in the lake." I feel stupid saying this out loud, particularly as I have no idea who I'm saying it to.

A pause. I wonder if she heard me. A heavy wind gust shakes the dry leaves of a large oak that towers overhead.

"Okay, but we're closed. You're trespassing."

Footsteps crunch on the sand as she approaches. The flashlight bounces loosely, sometimes directed at me and sometimes up into nothingness. She looks young, I think; maybe her features are pretty. The face has all its parts anyway. With the flashlight lowered and reflecting off the sand and water's edge, her eyes glint.

"Sorry," I say, "I come here all the time to walk around the lake. I never realized it was a problem."

"I'm new. They told me to keep people away. It's not a big deal."

My chest is so tight it feels as if I might break a rib. Yet being so close feels intimate. I wish she would touch me.

"I can leave. Do you want me to get your canoe first?"

She laughs a bit too animatedly. "That's my job."

"Your job is to chase down escaped canoes?"

More laughter. This is nice. "You got it." She removes her tennis shoes and socks, throwing them haphazardly on the sand, and traipses into the water until it is up past the bottoms of her shorts. With the canoe's tie rope in her hand, she suddenly squeals and jumps. This is followed by a frantic burst back to shore.

"What's wrong?"

"Something wrapped around my leg! Like a snake or tentacle or something."

The way her utility belt hangs off her hips looks comical: much too large and sliding down her hips. It strikes me more like a Halloween costume version of a guard uniform.

"I'm sure it was just a fish. The lake is stocked with catfish, trout, and some sunfish. Snakes here don't really swim underwater."

My attempt to allay her fears doesn't appear to work. I am coming off as weird. Awkward. The stupidest things erupt from my mouth.

"Not sure that's true, but I'm okay. Thanks for spotting the canoe. I'm going to head back, get this tied up."

The idea of losing this opportunity turns into a lead ball in my gut. *Please no*, I think. "Would you like to see my house?"

She stops cold. A gust thrashes the oak and all the trees surrounding the lake. It becomes so loud my ears ring. Terror climbs up my body like a rising thermometer. My thumb rubs the bracelet, the three intertwined braids. The house meant for this to happen, meant for me to meet her. It is obvious. This has to be.

She looks around the lake in an absent way. "Did you know that the sound of wind blowing through the trees is called psithurism?" Her voice, though sweet and melodic, is loud enough to be heard over the wind without shouting. It is as if it just appears in my head.

Now that it has a name, I listen to the wind blowing through the leaves for the first time. I study the elements of her face. Blonde hair flings itself in Medusa-like chaos. "It's a fun word. Kind of relaxing. Both the word and the sound."

"What's your name?" Her posture implies she is ready to shoot me.

"Killian."

"Hi. Sophia. Where do you live?" The quick rhythm of our conversation tenses me even more. I can't tell if she is being playful or antagonistic. I rub the bracelet desperately, hoping it will work like a gold lamp and something magical will happen.

"Up there. You see those lights? That's my house."

She does look up through the fall trees to the house on the hill, the deck lit up and living room set to red, as if expecting a murder. The house watches us from afar.

"Oh, right. I know who you are, Mister Gerard."

"You do?"

"Of course. Everyone does. And thank you for the offer, but maybe another time. Have a good night."

She grabs the canoe's line and turns. The canoe scrapes the bottom for long stretches. At the dock, she has to climb the embankment and circle back on the pier while still holding the rope. The canoe follows her along the pier and then around. There are always six on a side; I can see the ones tied on this side. When she disappears around the hut to tie up the loose one, I slip into the car.

"Drive around the lake and put my window down."

"Did you enjoy yourself?" she asks.

"Just drive."

The car backs out and turns left on Greenbriar Parkway. It winds through a valley between my mountain and Dead Man's Peak to the east. As we pass the marina, I catch sight of Sophia entering the hut. On this side, I count: one, two, three, four, five, six, seven. Thirteen boats. A bolt of energy shoots up my spine.

"There should only be twelve."

A motorcycle speeds by us. Its loud rumble hurtles across the lake, loud even above the soft wind that blows through my window. Twelve boats. Now thirteen. This makes no sense. Someone has put a thirteenth boat, an imposter, on the water.

I wave, thinking Sophia cannot see me. To my surprise, a woman reemerges, maybe drawn by the motorcycle's muffler roar. It must be her, there wouldn't be two young security guards to protect a nighttime lake. The woman waves back. Maybe everything will be okay.

"Drive as long as you can."

"I'll turn around when we reach the end of the parkway."

She always knows what's best for me.

A single bulb burns dimly overhead. Rafters hold paddles and life preservers and a broken boat so old its wood flakes off. Four cluttered sets of shelves run along two aisles to the right. To the left is the front counter. Pamphlets, advertising newsletters, and bins of knickknacks line the space. An old-style cash register rests at the end.

The wind gusts suddenly and forcefully, rattling the hut. The trees that ring the lake emit loud, white noise. From inside, it has the effect of sounding ghostly. Beside the cash register, a glass orb rests atop a three-pronged stand. Within rests a replica of the lake and marina. I pick it up.

"This is nice."

"Why are you here, Mister Gerard?"

I give the globe a firm shake. Ragged bits of brown leaves twist in a miniature cyclone. The whole time I play with it, Sophia's stare grows more intense.

"Is this what you intended?" I speak directly to the bracelet, as if it might answer me.

Sophia reaches for and produces a black can of pepper spray, to my dismay. The globe goes back on the counter. She is better illuminated now. Dirty blonde hair, beautiful all on its own, with slight curling around her neck. Her face does have all its parts. Someone once said that to understand how a person with face blindness sees others, turn pictures of people upside down. You know it's a face, but it looks foreign, not something you would recognize again. I have no idea if this is true but think about it whenever I have to look at another person.

The part about snatching Sophia and sneaking her back to the house brings no pride. The house willed it and ordained the car to stop, so I must obey. It wants something for me that I cannot acquire on my own.

"I will spray you if you don't leave. Right in the face."

"You know," I say, bolstered by the confidence the bracelet provides, "I love this time of year. This little heat wave has me sweating, but the leaves will all be gone soon. We'll have pumpkins and stew for dinner."

She turns her head half to me, making me unsure if she's staring back in the periphery or if something else in the shop has gained her attention. In a swift motion, the hand with the pepper spray raises, the nozzle directed at my face. My hand seizes the wrist and thrusts the weapon away just as it squirts. A cloud of vapor forms as close to her as me, and a draft blows it back into her face. Though the burn takes a moment, her reaction is violent: bottle dropped, hands to cover eyes, sudden red blotches across the evenness of her facial features.

"You motherfucker!" Her voice is no longer sweet.

I walk behind the counter and seize her waist. "I'm sorry. This is what the house wants." My remorse does nothing to calm her.

Count: one, two, three, four, five random business cards for local businesses taped to the counter's top. None of them are familiar to me. By the time I've scanned the text on each, my hand secures her mouth. Though the seven canoe side of the hut is not the side with the security light, that nearly full moon makes me feel conspicuous to carry her to the car, her arms and legs thrashing. No vehicle headlights show on the long loop of the parkway, though, so we make our escape.

The back passenger door swings open. I push her in first and then climb in. "Home."

"I'll pull into the garage when we arrive." The car's voice is so calming. Always. Every time. As if nothing at all could be wrong, implying this plan will go exactly to specifications. I feel so lucky.

Sophia immediately tries the door handle. It does not budge. Then she kicks me repeatedly, so many times my thigh and ribs feel bruised. To her right, a steep embankment drops down. On my left, another embankment shoots up out of view.

My heart pounds. This moment, these series of moments since we met—only a short while but seeming so much more—have been invigorating. A kind of limbo has been created, a feathery place where our togetherness is a cocoon. Soon, there will be no secrets. All will be out in the open. That's what the house wants. My thumb goes to the bracelet.

"Let me out. I mean it, or I'm going to kill you."

"I have no control over it."

Her anger boils. She kicks more, one that connects to my face. Before I pass out, I have time to see the trees grow thicker and the evening sky blemished with only occasional blots of white cloud. Below, to Sophia's right, the valley is dark and nearly imperceptible; the lake might instead be a frosty meadow. The mountain rising beside me seems an impossibly large behemoth. And there, within reach: Sophia, like a sprite aglow with celestial aura.

I wake in the backseat with my lips bleeding and jaw sore to move. The other rear passenger door is open. The garage light remains on, and the door into the house hangs open. I stagger. Inside, the small room that connects garage to large pantry has debris—broom, mops, cardboard boxes—scattered across the floor. Likewise, the pantry, except there it is cans and boxes of food.

Sophia stands in the living room pounding on the glass door to the deck when I enter. Her body turns with fists forward. Her shoulders twist to provide torque.

"Go fuck yourself."

"I'm sorry about this."

Food is on the large counter that separates kitchen from living room. A charcuterie that I know is sourced from local farms, or that's what I'm told. A fine summer sausage sampler. A cured prosciutto paired with Carolina Reaper infused cheddar. And a molasses bacon and bleu cheese crumble. All served with garlic sourdough crostini. A Wonder Oaks Cabernet to pair. All of this information is simply present, me wired to the house; and the house able to perform anything it wants. I wonder if there are robots that emerge from the walls.

I open my palms in a gesture toward the meat and cheese tray and the bottle. She looks at me as if I've spoken an alien tongue. I grasp and extend the Wonder Oaks, the label showing an odd, red image of a wooden tower rising from a mountain peak, an ancient tree lording over it with skeletal fingers.

"What do you want?"

Single piano notes from Bartók's *Mikrokosmos* seep from the house's speakers. Such disquieting romance. I close my eyes and sway in place, though there is no discernible tempo.

"We can make our own story, you and me. I want to live with happiness and great joy. The house will provide it." I can't understand what she's trying to express with her eyes. "I have face blindness, so I can't read what you're thinking."

She chokes on a laugh. "What I'm thinking? You can't guess?"

"Oh, god!" I say, finally understanding what must be going through her head. "That's not it! I'm not going to hurt you."

She lunges at me, knocking the bottle to the floor and into a million shards doused with red. "Let me out of here, you fucking creep!"

"I just wanted to look at you and enjoy the wine. Please don't hurt me."

She does not hurt me. Instead, she screams when the lights in the living room turn red. She runs.

An owl hoots from the sloping hill thick with pines and gnarled oaks, and sweetgum, hickory, and poplar. I stare through the closed sliding doors across the deck. Maybe I've grabbed the wrong person; I am debating whether to ask her name. The worry is she would then think me crazy.

She stands at the base of the stairs. In her hand is the cheese cutter. Not much of a weapon, but anything used with the proper motivation can kill.

"Did you know there's a lunar eclipse tonight?" This sudden question puts her stance into further alarm. "Sophia?"

The woman tries the front door and finds it as solidly locked as a vault. When I approach, my hands up in a sign of surrender, she races up the stairs. The house will direct her then. That is a relief. As I take the stairs too, the speakers begin *The Blue Danube Waltz*. Ugh. The house knows I hate this. It must know something about the woman. Is it Sophia then?

At the top of the stairs, I try to express the deep love I am feeling. For a moment, it could be any time, any place.

"Yes, that's it. Up here. You'll see."

She backs up facing me, that weirdly curved and forked knife like an imp's barb. Past the second bedroom door. Approaching the third. I hear it click and watch it split open a hair. The hallways light switches from red to yellow. Not the most romantic effect, but it does paint a mood.

When the woman steps beside it, the third door swings all the way open. A light flicks on. I watch her turn. Frozen in terror. I think her mouth opens, am almost sure of it. She doubles over, hands swung outward to fix her internal gyroscope. I am scared she will pass out.

"What the fuck is going on?" she says. "Oh my god. Oh god."

"The house knows you. It loves us both."

Her mouth moves maybe—I am confused by the mechanizations of her face—but I hear only small popping sounds. Finally, she exhales a deep, mournful sigh. "Is that real? Did you drug me?"

"It's tangible. Real is a more difficult concept. Like this bracelet. I found it this morning in the hall here. Maybe the house meant to bring us together. And here we are. But I know it feels like you're dreaming."

"Am I?"

I move toward her quickly. The knife twists from her grasp with one hand; my other hand seizes a wrist. We both turn. A single overhead bulb dangles by exposed wires in the room. On the far wall, large, fleshy membranes squeeze between bare two-by-fours. Fibrous tentacles stretch between them. The viscera ooze a rust-colored fluid, so that they glisten. There are wall-sized lungs on either side that expand and contract in slow movements. They are the size of small cars. A heart is snug under the lung on the right and thumps at a steady pace. Now that we see it, the sound of it pumping hits our chests. Attached to the ceiling is a gritty mass like moist clay that bubbles with lumps and folds.

Surprisingly, the woman no longer struggles. "You're out of your mind."

I nod. "It's the house. It takes care of me. Now it will take care of you too."

"No." She puts her free hand to her mouth. "That isn't going to happen to me." The woman's voice is raspy, as if she has screamed for days.

A soft aluminum tube that runs across the ceiling and disappears into the space above the hallway whistles as the house takes a deep breath.

I don't see the fist coming. It connects with my temple, a brutal crunch that causes a quake in my head. Her hair sways across her shoulders in slow waves, as if in water, as she staggers up the hall. The scent of her floral perfume, which I had casually noticed earlier, now strikes me full force. It mixes elegantly with the oils on her skin.

"Sophia, don't leave!"

Her hands grope at the walls for balance. She stops in front of the second bedroom door. When she turns, her eyes are black as the night sky and as deep. This is not Sophia. I don't know what this woman is, but she opens the bedroom door. Just as I arrive, she clutches my shirt, twists with all her might, and flings me inside. The door slams behind me and disappears. There are dozens of bodies at attention crammed into the small room. The faces bring deep fear. I touch them. They are hard.

A room full of mannequins. "No!"

After I feel one's hard skin, I push it to the floor. They pile onto me, on the attack, stiff wrists and fingers jabbing my body. The weight is unbearable. I fight. Their faces are blank ovals, lacking even the correct building blocks. I think at least one of them grips my arms with a fully clenched hand. Count: one, two, three...a million. The window is open, though is so far away I know it's there only from the haze of moonlight and the swaying trees. When I move toward it, the hands claw at my eyes, and I hear growls. At the sill, head poked through the window, the fresh air is a relief. One leg through. As I sit half in/half out, the mannequins move like a school of fish, darting toward me in a frenzy. I swing my other leg out and jump.

The ground slopes markedly at my fall spot, causing me to tumble to the edge of the house. More scrapes to my already beaten body. At the front door, the house welcomes me through the speaker and opens the door. Inside, empty. No charcuterie. No Wonder Oaks. No woman. Did I go into the second bedroom? I must have gone for a stroll.

In my bathroom, moving in a stupor, I turn the showerheads to boiling and wait until steam hides the ceiling. I lay in a fetal position on the tile floor. On the *her* side counter, in the place I set it, the bracelet twists into a coil.

The marina hut shines. Within, a blonde woman busies herself with some menial task. Restocking the cash register paper maybe. She has not seen me sneak from car to sidewalk. It is difficult to say why, but her features are familiar.

A growing shadow cuts across the moon. Such a sky, full of wonder and strange beauty. I start counterclockwise, crouching to get past the hut's window. By the time I walk a quarter way around, a strong breeze blows.

Far back, the little hut all but disappears in the eclipse's reddish glow. A shadow moves lazily across the water. I recognize it instantly: that lonely, impossible thirteenth canoe has again escaped its mooring. It is too far to wade in, and I am not inclined to rescue it. Instead, I unsnap the bracelet and hold it in my palm. Very light, almost imperceptible. With a heave, I throw it into the lake. Its outline bobs on the surface; of course, it will not sink.

Above, the moon goes into hiding, and the whole of the sky seems to darken. A rupture, a sliver, something that slices the heavens through its center, exposes light so bright it makes the lake steam. Wind swirls, and all the remnant fall leaves bustle into dancing cyclones. But it doesn't sound like wind in the trees at all. It is a scream.

For the Night is Long and I am Lost Without You

Erica Ruppert

THE BLIND THING that was Dena stirred its hands in tight, proscribed circles and curves, moving the water in patterns she could only feel. She willed her eyes to stay shut against the temptation to read what she had written. What needed to see, would see. A film of oil rode the water's surface and coated her fingers as she trailed them. She was cold in the cave's still air, cold in the water. She repeated the patterns as her hands grew numb. Then she wrote the patterns a third time, slowly, so there would be no mistake.

"Femina. Coniunx. Mater Caeca," came the women's voices, slushy with echoes, and under them the sound of something heavy sliding over a smooth surface. She could feel the water around her ripple, rise, as if a large body had sunk beneath the surface. Her skin prickled in anticipation of something sliding over her, but nothing did. She strained to hear more but was left in silence. She stilled her hands, held her breath, waiting for a response. A click of metal on stone like the turn of a lock echoed, and a sense of great emptiness came over her in a wave. The task was finished.

The blind thing opened its eyes and, sighted, was Dena again. She had assumed she stood in darkness, but the space around her was bright with reflected light. The cave was not a cave, but a room made of glass. The stars above her shone like flecks of ice in a hard sky. They picked light from windowpanes and scrolling metal in flares and spangles. She stood up to her hips in the black water of an oblong, white-tiled swimming pool. Currents tickled her ankles. She imagined fish drifting past her in the darkness, giant, pale carp grazing the pool's mucky bottom.

She turned around carefully, wary of her footing. She could not see the speakers, her companions. Above her, the cold moon glowed with enough light to cast sharp shadows.

"Hello?" she called out. Her voice came back to her, weaker, softer.

Nothing answered.

She waded out of the pool. One wall of the great glass room was solid and familiar, shared with the main house. A plain door in that wall stood ajar, and she could see lamplight in the long hallway beyond. She had walked down that hall, to that door, many times, had often tried the handle. It had always been locked.

Dena felt loneliness sweep in like a breeze against her cheek. The women who had brought her here could not have left so suddenly or so silently. Yet she had no sense of anyone in the house beyond her. Surely Maggie was still about, Dena thought, back in her cool bedroom undoing her braids. She trembled, wary of crossing back over the threshold, in case her sense became truth. With a glance at the looming stars, she stepped forward.

As she entered the house the great swell of isolation washed over her and away. Far inside she heard the noise of the other women moving about as they put away the trappings of the ceremony. She broke through a veil of dusty cobwebs that had amassed in her absence, then trekked down the long hall to her room to change into dry clothes and help them set the house back in order for the coming day.

"Why did you come for me?" Dena asked.

"You heard the call."

Dena thought Livia was being purposefully dense. Livia was the oldest of the three women Dena usually thought of as The Sisters, although she did not suspect any relation. Livia's hair was pale blonde and twisted tightly up in a crown around her head. The severe style made her look like the crone she often acted, although she was probably barely forty.

"No," Dena said. "Why me? Why not one of you?"

"Because we were not called."

"But then how are you here?"

"Arrangements needed to be made," Livia said. "We knew in our times, so we came and learned what we needed to make a place ready for you." Livia folded her hands against her breasts. "Don't be so obstinate. You knew it, too."

Before she had found this new purpose, Dena considered herself a confessional surrealist poet. She supported herself as a university tutor to make time for her art. She lived sparingly. Several years earlier she had managed to publish a chapbook titled *Dissolution*, from which she would perform readings less and less occasionally.

Dark haired, fever-eyed Anna had attended Dena's last reading at the public library. There she had cornered Dena to flatter her and engage her with questions about her art. At the time Anna seemed interested and interesting. Avid, even. Anna had invited her to the gray mansion where she lived with a group of like-minded women. Hungry, Dena had come.

Dena read her poetry to the three women in the house, and in turn they had read from their books in a mash of English, mangled Latin, and a wet, spongy language Dena had never heard before. At first, she had thought the women over-dramatic, fabulist, slightly mad. But there was a strange pull to what they said to her in their many voices, like something lonely crying without hope of friendship. She took her turn reading their books, even when the words were too thick for her tongue to manage and the meaning made her eyes sting. But the women encouraged her, touched her hands as she held the books, gave her a place in their ritual. Her own writing changed under their influence, became dreamier, less studiedly clever, and more wishful. Eventually, she stopped writing altogether and only read, although she was never quite sure she understood.

Dena moved in, seeking clarity. It always escaped.

Her quest to grasp how they defined their answers still seemed romantic then, allowing her to inhabit their city-wrapped mansion like distant royalty. But the bloom of such romance faded with time and familiarity and became rote demonstrations of an assumed faith. Dena admitted to herself in secret that it was an easier path than chasing poetry.

"Why are the prayers in Latin? I imagined something…older. Less churchy," she said.

Livia stirred the soup. "What's older than a dead language?"

Dena laughed, but Livia only watched her through the steam with a curious twist to her mouth.

"And what about the nonsense chant, how old is that?" Dena asked, still laughing.

"Do you think we invented this?" she said at last when Dena had quieted. "Do you think we invited you in because we are your friends?"

Dena knew she dreamed, knew that she flailed in her bed alone in the clinging darkness. Her mouth felt full of dust, burying her voice. The sheets bound her in place, and she struggled to be free of their damp clutch.

Under her digging hands the bedding was not cloth. Slippery, cold, what she touched was flesh that gave like a sopping sponge where she tried to grip it, too slick for her to hold. The chill of it frightened her, but she was too late to refuse the embrace tightening around her hips and her waist.

The cold pressed into her, heavy, distending her belly as the pulpy mass flowed up. Her skin split like an overripe melon, too big, too full. What spilled out was not formed, its gleaming black skin ebbing and flowing with a quick pulse. The amorphous product flowed away from her, seeking escape, surging against the door. Dena sat up, dreaming and awake.

The thing that crouched trembling on the doorstep could not be real. Flesh could not be bent that way. Black and decorated with the glimmer of stars.

Dena screamed against the muffled weight of her own tongue, choking on the cold threads and tendrils rolling over it. The air rippled around her. She was alone in her room.

"It's time now," Anna said. "We've waited. He's waited."

"How long?" Dena said.

Anna looked at her sideways. "Time isn't measured like that."

Dena put her head down.

"How many before me, then?"

Anna folded the towel and smoothed it as she put it in the drawer. "I don't know. The records only go back so far. The last before you was in 1871. The last time the time was right. Before then, I think in the seventeen hundreds, maybe before."

Dena nodded. We want to give a history to things, she thought, that are too young to bear any responsibility.

"Has this ever succeeded?" she asked.

Anna stopped her hands' nervous motion. "Once. But not here."

The Sisters told her the ritual had taken, that the time had been right. They read their books, studied the motion of the stars, and were certain. Dena accepted their answer as truth. It was easy.

She lay in the darkness with her hands on her flat belly, sure she felt something turn within her. How fast would her passenger grow, she wondered, this foreign seed, this godling.

The house around her was as silent as the mystery within her. Even if one of The Sisters had been awake to ask, they would not have any more of an answer.

Instead of becoming full and fleshy, Dena grew so spare that her ribs cast shadows beneath them. What she fed within her took everything and searched for more. Dena could feel what she carried moving through her, sometimes, like a quick-growing vine. Other times it was utterly still, and she a walking shell.

Gray-eyed Maggie brought her porridgy broth and heavy stews, trying to keep the weight on her. "It's no good if you can't survive to the birth," she said, practical, devout. Dena ate, but the thing in her ate more.

"There's nothing there," she said to Maggie one gray afternoon, afraid of her sunken belly.

"Sometimes there isn't," Maggie said. "It'll be back."

Dena kept her hand flat against the drum of her skin. How could you ever know, she thought, sadder than not.

"Are you and Anna sisters?" she asked suddenly, as if the question had been waiting behind her thin lips.

Maggie laughed then, a real laugh, and Dena could see a bright sliver of who she once had been.

"Not us," Maggie said. "Despite the hair color and the freckles. Just one of those coincidences that happen if something goes on long enough."

The clouds thinned and opened in an oval; framed and veiled within them was the thin disk of the moon against the gray afternoon light. Dena gazed at it from a tall, uncurtained window, unsettled and restless.

The Sisters came and went as they pleased and made no restrictions on her, but Dena preferred to stay in the confines of the house. She even avoided the small ornamental garden on the western side. The closeness of the plants, the dry enveloping stalks bounded by high iron fencing, made her feel claustrophobic.

Instead, she walked the mansion's wide halls to stave off boredom and contempt, watching autumn rot into winter in the park across the boulevard. She could not remember seeing spring come, or summer. The light through the tall windows seemed always dulled by clouds. Occasionally she saw a car pass, or a pedestrian stroll by, but the activity was all far removed from her. The window glass kept her safe and separate from whatever else went on in the world. Dena remembered the other side of the glass, the sounds, the scents, the noises, and clatter of other people. She didn't miss the cacophony, didn't miss the demands on her attention, the mundane expectations. But she thought it strange that she was so often left alone, when the house had promised company. An ill-tempered loneliness dogged her. Dena disliked the other women as much as she disliked the solitude.

She laced her fingers over the hollow between her hip bones and kept walking.

Her knees and elbows were great knots on her skinny limbs as what she carried grew. She felt like a knobby root, waiting to push out a pale tendril when the soil warmed enough. This was not the promised glow of coming motherhood. This was purely gestation.

Dena thought it was another dream at first, of the strange, holy birth sweeping through her like some terrible storm. Then the wracking cramps hit her, and she vomited over the side of the bed. She got up as the cramps eased, careful not to step in her own mess.

"Livia? Maggie?" Her voice was too thick to carry. She needed to get The Sisters. She needed help. There were still rites to be done.

The pain bent her like hot wire, clots and black fluid sluicing from her to splash on her feet. She dropped to the floor like a dead bird, the cold tiles soothing to her feverish skin. The stabbing pain ebbed away. She had the deep sense that this was not a birth at all.

Dena crawled until she reached a wall and used it to stand. "Maggie? Anna? Anyone, please," Dena called. Her own voice echoed back to her.

She held herself up with the wall and made her way out into the hallway. Cobwebs hung like shadows from the corners. The boards beneath her feet were soft with dust. Time measured itself differently here.

Her shadow crawled ahead of her like a spider.

The pain was less now, with her belly empty. An alien instinct urged her down the hallway, to the door. Tonight, the door was not locked. She twisted the knob and let herself fall into the cool, bright darkness.

The place was abandoned. The windowed walls and roof had cracked and fallen, leaving the pool exposed to the night and the icy stars. Dena lay still for a moment, drawing in deep breaths of the damp air. Shards gritted under her. Her nightgown was soaked in black blood and clung to her legs like swaddling. She peeled the cloth away from her skin and made herself stand again.

The ritual had its demands. She was past refusing them. Her stick-thin legs shook under her as she walked around the edge of the pool.

The pool was almost empty, drained to a sheet of liquid over a thin black muck. Still, the glassy stars shimmered on the oily surface, the baleful moon floated there. She walked silently through the empty space, shadows flowing before her like mercury. Broken glass scattered across the pool room's tiles, and she tread carefully to miss the shards. Still, unseen slivers drew blood, and her path was traced in red.

She looked up through the shattered roof panes at the true moon, the real stars. There was no comfort there, only the promise of endless cold.

Despite the water's level, ripples lapped against the sides of the pool with a metronome's beat, ringing dull cadence in the hushed night. The even tempo lured her with its calmness, and Dena stepped down into the slippery mess. It covered her to the knees as she walked down the inclined floor, deeper than she had judged.

Dena stood in the greasy water, letting the ripples lap against her wasted legs. She could understand the pattern in the ripples. She had written them herself, had felt them flow around her, and knew what they called. She shuddered. Tears welled up in her eyes, provoked by a slippery new fear. It was too late to flee back to the house. She still stood in the pool when the call was answered.

The metal frame of the room trembled and warped and gave before its coming, and she screamed, choking on spittle.

Sudden light blinded her, pouring from the high moon like water surging over a fall. Sharp fragments of glass still trapped in their frames crumbled in the weight of the light and fell over her like dry snow.

The white light splashed over her like acid, and she felt the brilliance eat into her skin, run down her bones. Dena thought she was still screaming but she could not hear her own voice. She lost her footing, fell with a splash into the shallows. Her throat swelled and tore as the light slid in, slick and cold as the water. She felt her lungs fill, and the chambers of her heart. The light looked out of her failing eyes at the pool, at the glass, at the wide night above, and receded like the tide.

The husk that had been Dena lay in the empty silence, a blind thing in truth, the greasy water dissolving what little was left after the light was gone.

Livia opened the door from the house slowly, ready to speak the words that barred it against the endlessly hungry thing she served. But the pool room was as still as ages. Stars flickered in the sky, making patchwork of Dena's empty bones.

This had not been her time.

"AUTOPSY ON A PUPPET": THE DAY OF LOST ILLUSION IN THOMAS LIGOTTI'S "MAD NIGHT OF ATONEMENT"

Chris Brawley

Naked apes or incarnate angels we may believe ourselves to be, but not human puppets.

—Thomas Ligotti

Who can know the intention of the Creator?

—Thomas Ligotti

Introduction: Puppet-Reality
"A wooden head opens strange worlds."[1] This passage from Kenneth Gross' *Puppet: An Essay on Uncanny Life* serves as the foundation of this essay. Although Gross' text is an exhaustive academic study of the history of puppets, the haunting atmosphere of his work portrays someone who knows more than just the academic side of puppets: he *knows* the uncanny life of puppets. He speaks of the "madness" of puppets, that they are "prophet-demons," waiting to speak a terrible truth about humanity, a truth too terrible to know. Puppets are from a "puppet reality" lying in wait to tell the world how puppet reality is related to our own supposed reality. Don't look too closely

---

[1] Kenneth Gross, *Puppet: An Essay on Uncanny Life* (Chicago: University of Chicago Press, 2012), 4.

at a puppet, Gross argues, because it will look back; And it may just begin to share its secret knowledge.

For Thomas Ligotti, puppets speak as well. In "The Puppet Masters," one of his vignettes in *Noctuary*, the narrator sits on a stool in the middle of a room, with puppets strewn about on the ground: in chairs, in the fireplace, and in and under the bed. He listens to them because he says they have lived through things unimaginable, and they are always speaking. The narrator listens to "histories and anecdotes of existences beyond the comprehension of most."[2]

Whether explicit or implicit, Ligotti's stories are filled with puppets, dolls, mannikins, and other human simulacra. They are, he admits, "the quintessence of the uncanny."[3] The purpose of the present paper is to analyze various aspects of Ligotti's puppet-reality, in particular as they are presented in "Mad Night of Atonement." Ligotti's use of puppets not only creates an uncanny *atmosphere* but leads to a question: whether or not humans are, in themselves, puppets. Aiding this discussion, equally applicable to his philosophical worldview and his fiction, Ligotti draws on both the Gnostic idea of the malevolent demiurge and the Buddhist concept on no-self (anatta); although these two philosophical systems seem to be points of departure for Ligotti, he arrives at a very different conclusion: there is no final salvation within these philosophical systems, there is only despair. The ultimate knowledge (gnosis) in Ligotti's work, "the secret to terrible to tell," is that humans are puppets, literally; free will is an illusion, and the "Day of Lost Illusion," (a phrase taken from Ligotti's story) is an *apocalypse*, when humanity finally realizes these truths. "Mad Night of Atonement" is the culmination of all these philosophical threads and is one of the most truly nightmarish stories of Ligotti's oeuvre.

The Uncanny
In many of his interviews, Ligotti shows a preference for the term "uncanny" in relation to his works. What exactly is meant by the uncanny? According to Nicholas Royle, the uncanny is a "crisis of the proper,"; Furthermore, "it has to do with a strangeness of framing and border, an experience of liminality."[4] It is a state of unhomeliness or displacement (*unheimlich*). As Ligotti

---

[2] Thomas Ligotti, *Noctuary* (New York: Carrol and Graf, 1994), 171-72.
[3] Thomas Ligotti, "Re: Help?" Email. June 22, 2017.
[4] Nicolas Royle, *The Uncanny* (Manchester: Manchester University Press, 2011), 1-2.

says, it is an inherent sense of *wrongness*, an uncertain sense of the world, an uneasiness with who we are and what our place is in the world; it is, in essence, a mingling of the familiar and the unfamiliar. And this sense of the uncanny can occur at any point, in any place, either in fiction or in real life. As an example of the uncanny occurring in real life, Professor Nobody (a pseudonym for Ligotti) has us ponder the following in "The Eyes that Never Blink": imagine you are sitting in a commonplace waiting room. Everything seems to be normal: the clock is ticking, people are talking, light is falling through the blinds. But then the "bunkers of banality" start to crumble, we think we see something in the corner; we have a strange sensation of something we cannot quite pinpoint. What it is we cannot say, but it evokes a sense of the uncanny within the ordinary, and this, according to Professor Nobody, is the ultimate horror that nothing can protect us from.[5]

In Ligotti's case, literature that invokes the uncanny is the most effective form of horror. Perhaps the best definition of what Ligotti means in terms of the uncanny is provided by Ligotti himself in an interview with Darrell Schweitzer: "the technique of delineating a condition of pervasive strangeness and unease is the approach I admire most in horror fiction."[6] Ligotti is a master of the uncanny, as are many of the authors he frequently refers to in interviews, writers such as Edgar Allan Poe, Vladimir Nabokov, or Bruno Schulz, whose impressionistic prose style is evocative—vague in details but one that has a powerful, dream-like effect on the reader.

Prior to Royle's full-length study of the uncanny, two of the most significant essays on the uncanny are "On the Psychology of the Uncanny" by Ernst Jentsch, and the more popular "The Uncanny" by Sigmund Freud.

Similar to Royle's view of the uncanny as a "crisis of the proper," Jentsch argues that the feeling of the uncanny suggests a *lack of orientation* in relation to things or incidents. Jentsch points out that the mind is most comfortable with what is "usual," experiences that occur every day; however, when a new or usual circumstance occurs, the mind approaches it with mistrust or even outright hostility (what he refers to as *misoneism*). The example Jentsch uses is the rising of the sun. We know from a very early age that there is nothing unusual about the sun rising every morning. However, when the

---

[5] Thomas Ligotti, *Conspiracy Against the Human Race: A Contrivance of Horror* (New York: Penguin Books, 2018), 133-34.

[6] Darrell Schweitzer, "*Weird Tales* Talks with Thomas Ligotti," in *Born to Fear: Interviews with Thomas Ligotti*, ed. Matt Cardin (Burton, Michigan: Subterranean Press, 2014), 46.

disorienting knowledge occurs to us that the sun rising is not the result of the sun but of the Earth's movement around the sun, then that may lead to an experience of the uncanny. Although this example is quite prosaic, what is important is that knowledge of what seems to be "self-evident" or "known" may abruptly change when we question traditional knowledge. It is when intellectual uncertainly as to the true nature of reality surfaces that the uncanny arises.

Jentsch points out that one of the most powerful (and fairly regular) experiences of intellectual uncertainty is when there is confusion as to whether an object is animate or inanimate. Thus, objects such as wax figures, dolls, automatons, or in Ligotti's case, puppets, can lead to a feeling of the uncanny. In art, of course, it takes a considerable talent to give the reader a feeling of the uncanny as it relates to human simulacra. Foremost among the literary masters of this effect is, of course, E.T.A Hoffman, specifically in "The Sandman", which is referred to not only by Jentsch, but also Freud in his exhaustive study of the uncanny, and of course by Ligotti himself.

The plot concerns itself with Nathaniel who, at an early age, hears the story of the Sandman, a figure who steals children's eyes and takes them to the moon to feed his children. As the story progresses, the Sandman gets associated with a family friend, Coppelius, and later Nathaniel's father dies as a result. Nathaniel then has a strained relationship with Clara, and then later, when he is off at university, he falls in love with Olympia, whom he later discovers is an automaton created by Spalanzani and another character, Coppola. After spending some time in an asylum, Nathaniel is almost healed. At the end of the story, however, Nathaniel thinks he sees Coppola when he's on a roof with Clara. He gets triggered, and after a failed attempt to throw Clara off the building, Nathaniel plummets to his death, his last words, "Beautiful eyes-a! Beautiful eyes-a!"[7]

In his essay "The Uncanny," Freud is also concerned with the aesthetic experiences of the uncanny. Freud agrees that Jentsch is partly correct, that the uncanny does relate to the doubt as to whether something is animate or inanimate; however, Freud argues that Jentsch does not take his argument far enough and that his analysis doesn't get to the real reason for the feeling of the uncanny. For Jentsch, what makes "The Sandman" story uncanny is the intellectual uncertainty as to whether Olympia is a real woman or an

---

[7] E.T.A. Hoffman, "The Sandman," *The Golden Pot and Other Tales* (Oxford: Oxford University Press, 1992), 118.

automaton. And, as Jentsch argues, this is one of the most common uses of the uncanny. So, for Jentsch, the doll itself is that which makes the story uncanny; for Freud, on the other hand, what makes the story uncanny is the connection between being robbed of one's eyes (the original locus of fear in the story of the actual Sandman that is told by the nurse), and the unconscious connection to the fear of losing one's genitalia (the castration complex).

There are connections to be made between Freud and Jentsch. After discussing the various etymologies of the word uncanny, including the similar words *weird*, *eerie*, *uneasy*, *unfamiliar*, or *gloomy*, Freud points out that what surrounds *heimlich/unheimlich* is not only what is familiar or unfamiliar, but what is *concealed* or *out of sight* (emphasis mine). So, *heimlich* is also that which is obscure, hidden from our normal knowledge, and something which *should* remain hidden but is not.

Freud also discusses the connections between "primitive man" and the infantile. In humanity's ancestral past, omnipotence of thoughts or wish-fulfillment would have been part of a common worldview. In the modern world, we know better. We have a more scientific worldview, but we still don't feel entirely comfortable with it; thus, any time something happens that reminds us of our old way of thinking, it can evoke a feeling of the uncanny. Not only is this connected to "primitive man" but it also connects to infantile complexes and animistic views of the world. The following quote by Freud concerning how the uncanny presents itself is relevant here: "An uncanny experience occurs either when repressed infantile complexes have been revived by some impression, or when the primitive beliefs we have surmounted seem once more to be confirmed."[8]

One can discern two ideas from Jentsch and Freud that may help shed light on the uncanny and Ligotti's work: one, an ontological uncertainty between the animate and inanimate (in life or art), that leads to a sense of the uncanny; and two, when something that is repressed or unknown comes to light, it carries with it a questioning of the very grounds of who we are and what our relationship to reality really is.

---

[8] Sigmund Freud, *"The Uncanny"* in *The Monster Theory Reader*, ed. *Jeffrey Andrew Weinstock (Minneapolis: University of Minnesota Press, 2020)*, 80.

The Uncanny Valley

Although concise and concerning itself with robotics, Masahiro Mori's essay "The Uncanny Valley" helps in the understanding affinities (or lack thereof) with human simulacrum and their relation to the uncanny, discussing not only robots, but puppets, toys, zombies and even corpses. He graphs how a human likeness, such as a puppet, relates to the affinity one has towards it. As an example, Miro discusses a prosthetic hand. Outwardly, a prosthetic hand can have such a sense of likeness that one hardly takes notice. However, if one was to grasp the prosthetic hand, with its lack of temperature or movement, the experience would become uncanny. So, even though the hand has a high degree of "human likeness," the "affinity" drops (hence the uncanny valley) due to the degree of the uncanny experience.

Complications arise with the addition of movement in a human simulacrum. Thus, in terms of a "healthy person," obviously human likeness and movement are at a high, but once a "healthy person" is deceased, uncanniness arises. So even though the likeness is there, the lack of movement lowers the affinity, dropping it even lower into the uncanny valley.

In relation to puppets, Miro points out that Bunraku puppets have a high level of human likeness (even though they are scaled down in size), and there is a high level of affinity for them, even more so because of the art involved. If Ligotti's use of puppets were taken into consideration, this is where he would disagree; with puppets there is no affinity. Whether there is movement or not, puppets are *always* uncanny and would be better placed at the lowest point in the uncanny valley. Even though humans and puppets are similar, they represent what Miro calls a "proximal form of danger," perhaps an evolutionary advantage protecting humans from that which is too similar. What Miro refers to as the proximal form of danger is exactly what Ligotti wishes to express in his stories concerning puppets.[9]

Gnosticism

In *The Soul of the Marionette: A Short Inquiry into Human Freedom,* John Gray argues that if puppets were ever to achieve self-awareness, their religion would be Gnosticism.[10] Referring to Heinrich von Kleist's famous essay "On the Marionette Theater," Gray points out that the *grace* Kleist gives his

---

[9] Masahiro Mori, "The Uncanny Valley" in The Monster Theory Reader, 94.
[10] John Gray, *The Soul of the Marionette: A Short Inquiry into Human Freedom* (New York: Farrar, Straus and Giroux, 2015), 9.

puppets is due to their lack of choice; in contrast, however, humans are subject to the burden of choice, thus making them flawed creatures. Humans have eaten from the Tree of the Knowledge of Good and Evil and are impure beings always burdened with choice. Kleist's final point (as made through a dialogue) is that one day purity will appear either as something with no consciousness (a puppet), or consciousness without limit (a God). The hope, then, is that in the end humanity will be restored to its original unity with God, a view Gnostics championed. As we shall see, however, although Ligotti does share some of the Gnostic views pointed out in Kleist, in the end, for Ligotti, there is only horror.

With regards to Gnosticism, scholars such as Bart Erhman, Elaine Pagels, and David Brakke have reminded us that there was such diversity within the early forms of Christianity that it is impossible to talk about a single, unified Church. Christianity as we know it today did not exist, nor was there a competing, heretical religion known as the "Gnostics" that eventually "lost out." Instead, the Gnostic school of thought was just one of the participants in a very enthusiastic "multilateral process" of emerging Christianity. The Gnostic school of thought flourished around the 2nd and 3rd centuries. It combined aspects of Platonism, alternate readings of Jewish scriptures, and complex meditations on the divine intellect for the purposes of salvation. It must be noted that scholars disagree on whether "Gnosticism" is a religion in the true sense of the word or if it is a loose amalgamation of disparate views of the world. Furthermore, it must be noted that coming up with a consistent theory concerning the Gnostics is an impossibility; difficulties include that, in reading the gospels, there is no consistent point of view shared by the texts; scholars cannot determine which of the texts were authoritative in any way; and the texts are so complex that it is difficult to reach a consensus as to how to actually read them.

Even if there are many studies *for* or *against* the use of "Gnosticism" as a religion, these arguments are unnecessary for our present purpose. So, although it is impossible to reach as consistent view of the Gnostics, they shared a belief that the way to salvation consisted of Gnosis (Greek for "knowledge"). In order to achieve this, the Gnostics did share some common features in their beliefs: the Jews do not have the "true" God, but only a lower form of God, a Platonic demiurge (referred to a Yaldabaoth), who was an incompetent creator of a world that never should have been; the figure of Christ reveals a way to ascend to the truth; and Christ is not a flesh and blood person but a symbol for the knowledge of salvation.

Up until the past one hundred years, the only information scholars could use to discuss the Gnostics were the critics of it, including Justin Martyr, Tertullian, and Irenaeus, whose *Against the Heresies* made outrageous claims such as midnight orgies or the eating of babies, accusations leveled at anything that was against their form of Christianity.

However, one of the most significant finds of the twentieth century occurred in 1945 in Nag Hammadi, Egypt. Thirteen ancient books were discovered in an earthen jar that, upon further investigation, proved to be gospels that were lost or forgotten. These books contained fifty-two literary works written in Coptic. These texts challenged the proto-orthodox views, and when they were translated, they offered the world a more comprehensive look at what the religious landscape of the time truly was.

The best inroad to Ligotti's "Mad Night of Atonement" is the central Gnostic text, the *Apocryphon of John*, a revisionist interpretation of Genesis and the most complete version of the Gnostic creation story.[11]

The basic myth in the *Apocryphon of John* describes "The One," a "God" or "Being" that is referred to as indescribable and indefinable. This being is similar to Eastern religious concepts such a *Brahman*, *Dao*, or even similar traditions of Western mysticism, as in the Kabbalah, Christian mystics such as Meister Eckhart, or the Sufi tradition in Islam. This indescribable divine being apprehends itself, such that two beings now emerge: God and God-aware-of-God. This splitting of the divine being continues until the pleroma ("fullness") of God manifests itself into many divine beings. Part of God's mind then splits again, and Sophia ("Wisdom" and referred to here as feminine) seeks out knowledge apart from the pleroma or fullness of the divine being. She then creates another being, a horrific demiurge by the name of Yaldabaoth. This monster has hopes of creating the world, but because of his lack of knowledge of the divine realms, he instead makes a poor imitation of the world. This world, according to the Gnostics, is the world as it is created in Genesis, a mere imitation of the divine realms; furthermore, it is the world in which humans experience suffering, hardship and death. The good news, according to the Gnostics, is that the world is finally restored through Jesus (referred to as "Forethought," or "the Entirety"). How it is restored is based on the secret knowledge (gnosis) that Jesus provides his followers. By knowing the faulty nature of the world created by Yaldabaoth,

---

[11] Stevan Davies, *The Secret Book of John the Gnostic Gospel: Annotated and Explained* (Nashville: Skylight Paths, 2005), x.

Gnostics could contemplate and finally achieve true knowledge of the divine realms.

As Stevan Davies points out in his translation of the *Apocryphon*, the Gnostic system is a "mind-model" of religion, similar to such religions as Buddhism or Hinduism. The history of the world is not viewed literally as actual events, but in reality, an unfolding of God's mind through history (the emphasis being more on the symbolic nature of the story and not historical veracity). The Gnostic revisionist myth of creation reveals what Davies describes as a "divine madness [that] receives psychotherapy that is the history of the world."[12]

Ligotti has himself said that Gnosticism was the "perfect fit" for his view of the universe, so the connections are interesting.[13] Although Ligotti is an atheist himself, he is at his most effective as a writer of supernatural horror when the device of the malignant demiurge is employed to show the purposelessness of life and the ignorance of those who look at the world with any degree of hope or salvation. Similarly, if one applies the "mind model" of the Gnostics as Davies suggests, it seems as if Ligotti's stories never transcend that of the malignant demiurge and always fail to offer any kind of salvific figure. There is no salvation at all, only the bleakness of being. In fact, when Ligotti discusses the supernatural horror as a genre, and those who have a certain taste for it, he says it's "a means for damaged psyches to express their experience in a damaged universe, or to find reflection of this experience in the writings of others"[14] and further that supernatural literature is "a metaphysical counterpart of insanity."[15] Applying the Davies' quote above to Ligotti, there is indeed a revelation of "divine madness"; what there is not, of course, is any type of psychotherapy because, for Ligotti, that would be patently insane nonsense.

Buddhism

Another angle to use to approach Ligotti's fiction is Buddhism. Throughout *The Conspiracy Against the Human Race,* and in his many interviews, Ligotti states that while Buddhism may not be "his point of departure," he shares a

---

[12] Ibid, 58.
[13] Thomas Ligotti, "Interview with TANK Magazine," *A Little White Book of Screams and Whispers* (Maryland: Borderlands Press, 2019), 45.
[14] Stefan Dziemianowicz, "Interview with Thomas Ligotti," *Born to Fear*, 39.
[15] Neddal Ayad, "Literature is Entertainment or It Is Nothing: An Interview with Thomas Ligotti," *Born to Fear*, 96.

similar view, namely that of Buddha's First Noble Truth: All life is suffering. However, similar to the argument concerning the Gnostics, Ligotti takes issues with many aspects of Buddhism. For example, there is a plan for salvation; after one sees through the world as one created by a "false" god, one is able to achieve a salvific knowledge that can bring about a oneness with the higher power. The other three Noble Truths of the Buddha say that there is a way out of suffering by following the Eightfold path, which gives the practitioner "awakening" and deliverance from rebirth.

It is easy to see how Ligotti departs from the Buddhist system. There is no final salvation at all, only suffering. And what exactly is Enlightenment anyway? And how many people actually achieve it? In Ligotti's passing reference to Ken Wilbur's book, *One Taste: Daily Reflections on Integral Spirituality*, when asked of a Zen Master how many were truly enlightened, the master put the number at a dozen; and, according to another master, the entire history of Zen Buddhism only shows one thousand who are truly enlightened.[16] Now, of course, there is no way to know if the numbers are accurate, but the point remains: whatever enlightenment is, there are not many people who achieve it. Further questioning of what exactly constitutes enlightenment, and whether it is real in any way, is a discussion of people who have claimed some such awakening: U.G. Krishnamurti, John Wren-Lewis, and Suzanne Segal. Suffice it to say, Ligotti leaves readers with much doubt as to whether any form of spiritual salvation is real.

One of the central tenants of Buddhism is the idea of anatta (no-self, no-soul). This is directly tied to the idea of suffering due to the fact that the more one identifies with a permanent self (as opposed to seeing it as the true illusion it is), the more this attachment to self leads one to suffering and continued rebirth in the cycle of samsara. The goal in Buddhism is to have a deep awareness that what we think of as reality is really just a magic trick, an illusion (Buddhist *maya*), and that to see through it leads to nirvana (literally, "to blow out"), a state of non-attached peace or bliss. So, as with the Gnostics or many other religions, there is salvation, there is a release from this horrible world of suffering if one can only get beyond the illusion of self.

The idea of no-self also has connections with neuroscience, specifically work done by Thomas Metzinger in *Being No One: The Self-Model Theory of Subjectivity* and *The Ego Tunnel: The Science of the Mind and the Myth of the Self*. Metzinger's main point is that there is no such thing as a "self": there is

---

[16] Ligotti, "Interview for *Noctuary*," *A Little White Book of Screams and Whispers*, 122.

no little man in our head who is "us" and who determines our actions. Or, as Ligotti effectively describes it: the world itself is like a carnival ride, where the ride is going, but there is nobody in the seat to experience it. What we are, according to Metzinger, are "selfing organisms" who have a *phenomenal self-model* (PSM) that he defines as "a distinct and coherent pattern of neural activity that allows you to integrate parts of the world into an inner image of yourself as a whole.[17] Through evolution, which is a blind force and subject only to chance, we have what is known as an Ego Tunnel, a filtering mechanism that allows us to experience a reality that is unique to us. It is, perhaps, unnerving to know that, for example, a red apple does not have an objective "red" color at all but only "appears" to the brain as red based on the integrative one-world model that correlates all of the information together.

Thus, consciousness according to Metzinger is only the *appearance of a world*, not a world in and of itself. So why do we not *know* this? Metzinger argues that the *phenomenal self-model* is transparent, meaning that we are unaware of how information about reality gets to us; it is like being able to see a bird through a window but not the window itself. In fact, one of the great evolutionary advantages of the transparency of the PSM is that it conceals the truth about the mechanisms of consciousness themselves. We are, what Metzinger calls naïve realists, in that we think we are in touch with an objective reality outside us, when the truth is that we are not. And that is a good thing. Metzinger states, "as long as nothing goes wrong, naïve realism makes for a very relaxed way of living."[18]

But what if something does go wrong? What if someone had the special ability, the knowledge (gnosis) to see beyond the Ego Tunnel? For Metzinger, and Ligotti as well, humans would realize that although we may be intelligent, we are not the result of intelligent design. We did not ask to exist or to suffer the way that we do, so if all that we experience is the result of neural wiring and an Ego Tunnel, then there is no "God" or outside power at all. In fact, even if there was such a God who created this world, for Metzinger that God would be "cruel and diabolic" or for Ligotti, "an incontinent dotard who soiled Himself and the universe with His corruption, a low-budget divinity passing itself off as the genuine article."[19]

---

[17] Thomas Metzinger, *The Ego Tunnel: The Science of the Mind and the Myth of the Self* (New York: Basic Books, 2009), 115.
[18] Metzinger, *The Ego Tunnel*, 46.
[19] Ligotti, *Conspiracy*, 116.

Dr. James Trafford has written on the comparisons between Ligotti and Metzinger in his essays "The Philosophy of Thomas Ligotti: *True Detective* and the Thoughts of an Obscure Literary Master" and "The Shadow of a Puppet Dance: Metzinger, Ligotti and the Illusion of Selfhood." Trafford refers to Ligotti's universe as a "suffocating irreverence for the world" that "infects the entire atmosphere of existence."[20] Anyone who has read Ligotti will notice this immediately. Ligotti, according to Trafford, turns the real world inside out to show that it wasn't even real in the first place. This is the result of the dark gnosis at the center of Ligotti's universe. If we were able to see beyond the Ego Tunnel, we would see the most terrible knowledge: that we are not selves, that there is a "perniciousness" behind the world, and that we are the result of our heredity and neural wiring. It is the terrible knowledge that we are puppets.

What is it that awaits when the veil of the world has been lifted? For Ligotti, it is not an awakening to anatta (non-self), it is an awakening to the true nature of the world: humans are mere puppets in a puppet show, controlled by unknown forces and headed towards the only salvation possible for humanity—suffering and death. Once this dark gnosis has been realized, humans come to realize that self-consciousness, the most malignant of all forces, has led to the awareness that we are in a world that is determined. The puppet, the prophet-demon, has finally revealed the true nature of the world: "this mechanism of wires determines everything we think, say, and do. There is nothing inside us that we can call us. Except by means of a common delusion, we are all puppets – period."[21]

Determinism

Sam Harris hypothesizes that if the scientific community determined beyond doubt that free will was nothing but an illusion, we would have a culture war far surpassing that of evolution.[22] For Ligotti, it would mean the breakdown of sanity itself. In Ligotti's story, "Mad Night of Atonement," the Day of Lost Illusion is the fictional realization that humans are puppets and everything is determined. One can see constant references in *Conspiracy Against the Human Race* to Schopenhauer's philosophy of the Will (or Will-

---

[20] James Trafford, "The Philosophy of Thomas Ligotti: *True Detective* and the Thoughts of an Obscure Literary Master" *The Critique*, July 15, 2015. http://www.thecritique.com/articles/the-philosophy-of-thomas-ligotti/
[21] Flakk, Pal, "Interview with Pal Flakk," *Born to Fear*, 210.
[22] Sam Harris, *Free Will* (New York: Free Press, 2012), 1.

to-live) as a blind force that keeps everything running. Only the force is real, not the people, and self-consciousness is what keeps us apart from nature and makes us believe we are in control when we are not. Ligotti considers himself to be a strong determinist, stating, "philosophical works on human behavior and emotions are causally determined, along with the absence of a core self, [and have] consolidated convictions of mine that may seem to be expressed by use of puppets in my stories."[23] For Ligotti, the puppets are the quintessence of the uncanny and of his pessimistic worldview, that "behind the scenes of life there is something pernicious that makes a nightmare of our world."[24]

The mechanistic, puppet-reality, combined with the uncanny, is also effectively considered at the end Jetsch's discussion of the uncanny discussed above. Here, Jentsch discusses epilepsy which, interestingly enough, is referred to as the sacred disease (*morbus sacer*) because it seemed as if this disease had its origin in some other world, that it was somehow so foreign to nature. Seeing the spasms of the human body can lead to an uncanny response for the ordinary person who is not used to seeing such phenomenon on a regular basis (like a nurse or a hospital setting). As Jentsch states, "the dark knowledge dawns on the unschooled observer that mechanical processes are taking place in that which he was previously used to regarding as a unified psyche."[25] So, as with Buddhism, no unified "self" really exists at all, and contrary to this leading to salvation, in Ligotti's work it leads to a dark awareness that we are nothing but bits and pieces, puppets.

Ligotti provides his own example of puppet-reality in an interview with Pal Flakk where he discusses anhedonia broadly and Terry Bradshaw specifically. Bradshaw, the Hall of Famer, admitted to never feeling a sense of pleasure at winning any of the Super Bowls. The reason for this, according to Ligotti, is that while Bradshaw was certainly in control of how great he was as a quarterback, he was not in control of his own mind; there was no reward-system in place to bolster his own self. Echoing his whole philosophy, Ligotti says that not only was Terry Bradshaw not in control of his brain, there really is no "Terry Bradshaw" in the first place. Beyond the façade of a unified psyche is only a system of wires. There is only a puppet.

---

[23] Thomas Ligotti, "Re: Help?" Email. June 22, 2017.
[24] Ligotti, *Conspiracy*, 38.
[25] Ernst Jentsch, "On the Psychology of the Uncanny" trans. Roy Sellars, http://www.art3idea.psu.edu/locus/Jentsch_uncanny.pdf, 14.

Mad Atonement

In an interview with TANK magazine, Ligotti humorously quotes Woody Allen: "If it turns out there is a God…the worst you can say about him is that he's an underachiever."[26] Furthering this sentiment, Ligotti admits that any creator who made this awful world we live in must be "mad" or "monstrous" and that this "God" should atone for his horrible creation (this is interesting given that Ligotti is an atheist). Thus, Ligotti's story, "Mad Night of Atonement: A Future Tale," successfully embodies all of the ideas discussed thus far: puppets and puppet-reality, the uncanny atmosphere created by the puppet, the half-truth of Gnosticism, the Buddhist idea of no-self, and finally the truth of Determinism. And, since Ligotti subtitles the story "a Future Tale," the Day of Lost Illusion is the day when humanity is impacted most fully by these ideas.

The Lecture

For simplicity's sake, the story contains two major movements: a lecture given by Dr. Haxhausen to explain his revelation and a demonstration of his machine.

Within the first few pages of the story, Ligotti uses many religious allusions. Explaining to his audience the reason for his long departure from the scientific world (in which some people thought he had gone mad), Dr. Haxhausen says he was given a "Revelation," "the world was to be given notice, an annunciation made," and he was to "spread the word." Furthermore, Dr. Haxhausen makes it clear to his audience that he is not the Almighty, but that he was given these revelations by the Almighty and "in no uncertain terms received an itinerary of action from the same source."[27] It's telling that Ligotti uses "itinerary of action." What exactly is the "itinerary of action" that Dr. Haxhausen receives?

Before the story delves into this itinerary of action, Dr. Haxhausen describes an encounter with the Creator. In one of the uncanniest images in all of Ligotti's fiction, Dr. Haxhausen sees the Creator in an abandoned warehouse. Amidst the darkness and ruins, Dr. Haxhausen sees a form crumpled up in a corner, with legs like a cripple and two eyes peering out "like colored

---

[26] Ligotti, "Interview TANK Magazine," *A Little White Book*, 45.
[27] Thomas Ligotti, "Mad Night of Atonement," *Noctuary* (New York: Carrol and Graff), 108.

glass in the moonlight."²⁸ The form speaks to him not in a peaceful or consoling manner, but instead in sad and inarticulate "moans." The ultimate "revelation" here is that Dr. Haxhausen has a true theophany: the Creator is a simple and sad department store mannikin. This has obvious parallels to the Gnostic reinterpretation of Genesis: the "True" God of the Gnostics is a malignant demiurge who created a false world filled with suffering.

What Dr. Haxhausen learns, and what he promotes to his audience, is that humans have gone against the Creator's will completely and have gotten life all wrong. For Haxhausen, humans have mistakenly seen life as something that is inherently "good," something benevolent that evolves into something even better, every day. Humans, for Dr. Haxhausen, are so focused on paradise that they do not see the flaws of creation. There is a failure to take into account corruption and to understand that the only true destiny is disintegration. Not only that, but humans think that this constant evolution towards perfection is all part of a bigger plan, God's plan. This is what everyone believes to be the truth. What Haxhausen learns from the Creator, however, is exactly the opposite. Contrary to life getting better and better, all that exists is nothing but ruins. It is likened to an old, abandoned fairground, which one sees off of a dirt road, a ghostly place of "broken booths" and "sagging tents."²⁹ Although the imagination attempts to revive the old fairground, to see it again in all of its splendor, it cannot. And this, Haxhausen says, is where people fail to see the truth. The true destiny of all things is ruin, disintegration and decay. Haxhausen teaches that the whole time humans have "erred on the side of excellence," they have failed to notice that "all the Creator had in mind was a third-rate sideshow of beatific puppetry."³⁰ It is this awareness, both in this particular story and in Ligotti's worldview, that leads one to a dark gnosis, the knowledge that contrary to what humans see or think they see, there is something "pernicious" going on behind the scenes, a secret too terrible to know.

The Demonstration
The demonstration Dr. Haxhausen provides is directly related to the "Revelation" he has had from the Creator. It is a great machine, made up of all sorts of odds parts, including alembics, swords, bells, and, of course, dolls

---

[28] Ibid, 112.
[29] Ibid, 113.
[30] Ibid, 116.

and puppets made out of wood and wax and looking like "malicious children in hiding."[31] At the top of this device, there is an old stovepipe that faces towards the sky, the "Sacred Ray" (the Creator's eye), which draws its power from the moonlight and brings about a conversion of sorts.

What is finally revealed is what Dr. Haxhausen refers to as the "Creator's Great Design" or "The Puppet Machine." On the stage, he places real audience participants (volunteers) along with various dolls and puppets on the stage. The backdrop to this display, in typical Ligottian style, is a drab mural with only black and white. Adding further to the uncanny effect of the show, Haxhausen has placed musicians on stage who are full-sized automatons (a violist and a concertina). As the music plays, Haxhausen points to what is happening on the stage: the human volunteers are turning into puppets, with the "wax and wood and shining glass to replace the sad and cumbersome structures of biology."[32] As the audience members look on in disbelief, some in anger thinking that doctor has gone mad, he explains to them that this change is only temporary, that no harm has been done, because the greatest sin would be to transform people into puppets without their choosing to do this willingly. The curtain lifts, the puppets turn back into humans, and the show is over.

Or is it? After it is mentioned that Dr. Haxhausen is found hanged (suicide? Murder?), there is a dramatic shift in point of view. The words are from the Creator himself:

> But of course you know, ladies and gentleman, what it was that happened. I can see by the glitter in your eyes, the flush on your waxen faces, that you remember well how the colors appeared in the night sky that night, a fabulous aurora sent by the sun and reflected by the moon, so that all the world would be baptized at once by the spectral light of truth. Willing or not, your hearts had heard the voice of the creature you thought mad. But they would not listen; they never have. Why did you force this transgression of divine law? And why do you still gaze with your wooden hate from the ends of the earth? It was for you that I committed this last and greatest sin, all for you. When have you ever appreciated these gestures from on high![33]

---

[31] Ibid, 106.
[32] Ibid, 116.
[33] Ibid, 118.

So, at last, the Creator is speaking to the world that, in contrast to there ever being a "willingness" to convert themselves into puppets, the Creator has done it for them, has taken on the "greatest sin" for which humanity is, of course, not even appreciative. This last action is similar in many ways to the work of one of Ligotti's biggest influences: Bruno Schulz. In fact, Dr. Sean Moreland's essay "Maddening Manikins: The Atmospheric Machines of Poe and Ligotti" makes the point explicit, showing how Ligotti creates an "uncanny sublimity and dread" by his use of "the psychic and literary sutures" between Poe and Schulz himself.[34] In a chapter of *The Street of Crocodiles* entitled "Treatise on Tailors' Dummies, Continuation," the mad father discusses the Demiurge and all of the possibilities inherent in matter itself. Referring to waxwork figures or fairground dummies, he asks: "Can you imagine the pain, the dull imprisoned suffering, hewn into the matter of that dummy which does not know why it must be what it is, why it must remain in that forcibly imposed form which is no more than a parody?"[35] He further discusses the "tyranny" imposed on the wood, and the "terrible sadism" involved in its shaping into form. So, this conclusion to "Mad Night of Atonement" essentially says that we *can* imagine the pain and dull imprisoned suffering of the dummy because that's exactly what we are. Although we think we have been blessed with consciousness, it has been our greatest curse; it is that which sets us apart from nature and is one of evolution's most destructive errors.

The final lines of the story have the reader questioning even the role of the Creator himself. As a form of petitionary prayer, the Creator says: "Oh, blessed puppets, receive My prayer, and teach Me to make myself in *thy* image."[36] In this line, does the Creator want to be a puppet? Is the Creator being sarcastic when praying to his creation? Are we the creation or is the Creator the creation? Are we puppets? Are we real? Can we "will" ourselves into action? And how can we if we are tangled in the strings?

Conclusion: Life as the Dream of a Puppet

There is a powerful parable in the work of the Daoist philosopher, Chuang Tzu. In the parable, Chuang Tzu has a such a powerful dream that he is a

---

[34] Sean Moreland, "Maddening Manikins: The Atmospheric Machines of Poe and Ligotti," *Vastarien: A Literary Journal* Vol. 2, Issue 3 (2019), 125-157.
[35] Bruno Schulz, "The Street of Crocodiles," *The Street of Crocodiles and Other Stories* (New York: Penguin Books), 35.
[36] Ligotti, "Mad Night," 118.

butterfly, that upon awakening he doesn't know if he was Chaung Tzu dreaming he was a butterfly or if he was a butterfly dreaming he was Chuang Tzu. This ontological confusion is similarly employed in many of Ligotti's greatest stories, and results in what Trafford describes as a discrepancy between realism and oneirism, between what is thought to be "real" and what is "unreal" or dreamlike.[37] This observation is important in understanding the effectiveness of Ligotti's work; the boundaries between "real" and "unreal" are always confused. What if life really is nothing but the dream of a puppet? What if the ontological confusion in Ligotti's fiction led to a "living confusion"? Wouldn't this be the most horrible truth to know?

Ligotti has said that "all apocalyptic phenomena take place on a personal level."[38] The uncanny atmosphere created by Ligotti's puppets opens up philosophical paths to madness for the individual, starting with the knowledge of the malignant Gnostic demiurge, who created a sad imitation of the divine realm, our present world of pain and suffering. Of course, as humans we will do anything to protect ourselves from this knowledge, pretending all the while that we are making a go of it on our own. But, as we know, the puppet always looks back at us and tells us the dark truths we do not want to admit to ourselves. In the end, Ligotti is the master ventriloquist: his puppets anxiously await as the Day of Lost Illusion slowly approaches.

---

[37] James Trafford. See footnote 12 in "The Shadow of a Puppet Dance: Metzinger, Ligotti and the illusion of Selfhood," *Collapse IV*, ed. R. MacKay (Falmouth: Urbanomic, 2008), 188-89.
[38] Matt Cardin, "It's All a Matter of Personal Pathology: An Interview with Thomas Ligotti" *Born to Fear*, 131.

BIBLIOGRAPHY

Angerhuber, E.M. and Thomas Wagner, "Disillusion Can Be Glamorous: An Interview with Thomas Ligotti" in *Born to Fear: Interviews with Thomas Ligotti*, ed. Matt Cardin (Burton, MI: Subterranean Press, 2014), 59-75.

Ayad, Neddal, "Literature is Entertainment or It Is Nothing: An Interview with Thomas Ligotti" in *Born to Fear: Interviews with Thomas Ligotti*, ed. Matt Cardin (Burton, MI: Subterranean Press, 2014), 95-116.

Brakke, David. *The Gnostics: Myth, Ritual, and Diversity in Early Christianity*. Massachusetts: Harvard University Press, 2010.

Cardin, Matt, "It's All A Matter of Personal Pathology: An Interview with Thomas Ligotti," in *Born to Fear: Interviews with Thomas Ligotti*, ed. Matt Cardin (Burton, MI: Subterranean Press, 2014), 117-133.

Davies, Stevan. The *Secret Book of John the Gnostic Gospel: Annotated and Explained*. Skylight Paths, 2005.

Flakk, Pal, "Interview with Pal Flakk," in *Born to Fear: Interviews with Thomas Ligotti*, ed. Matt Cardin (Burton, MI: Subterranean Press, 2014), 207-216.

Freud, Sigmund. "The Uncanny" in *The Monster Theory Reader*, ed. Jeffrey Andrew Weinstock, (Minneapolis: University of Minnesota Press, 2020), 59-88.

Gray, John. *The Soul of the Marionette: A Short Inquiry into Human Freedom*. New York: Farrar, Straus and Giroux, 2015.

Harris, Sam, *Free Will*. New York: Free Press, 2012.

Hoffman, E.T.A. "The Sandman," *The Golden Pot and Other Tales*. Oxford: Oxford University Press, 1992. 85-118.

Jentsch, Ernst. "On the Psychology of the Uncanny," trans Roy Sellars, http://www.art3idea.psu.edu/locus/Jentsch_uncanny.pdf, 1-16.

Ligotti, Thomas. *The Conspiracy Against the Human Race: A Contrivance of Horror*. New York: Penguin Books, 2018.

___. *A Little Book of Screams and Whispers*. Maryland: Borderlands Press, 2019.

___. *Noctuary*. New York: Carroll and Graf, 1994.

Metzinger, Thomas. *The Ego Tunnel: The Science of the Mind and the Myth of the Self*. New York: Basic Books, 2009.

Moreland, Sean. "Maddening Manikins: The Atmospheric Machines of Poe and Ligotti," *Vastarien: A Literary Journal* Vol.2, Issue 3 (2019), 125-157.

Mori, Masahiro "The Uncanny Valley" in *The Monster Theory Reader*, ed. Jeffrey Andrew Weinstock, (Minneapolis: University of Minnesota Press, 2020), 89-94.

Schulz, Bruno. *The Street of Crocodiles and Other Stories*. New York: Penguin Books, 1977.

Schweitzer, Darrell, "*Weird Tales* Talks with Thomas Ligotti" in *Born to Fear: Interviews with Thomas Ligotti*, ed. Matt Cardin (Burton, MI: Subterranean Press, 2014), 41-49.

Trafford, James. "True Detective and the Thoughts of an Obscure Literary Master." *The Critique: The Philosophy of Thomas Ligotti*, 2015.

___. "The Shadow of a Puppet Dance: Metzinger, Ligotti and the Illusion of Selfhood." *Collapse IV* ed. R. MacKay (Falmouth: Urbanomic, 2008), 188-89.

Deep Sea Creature

Vivian Kasley

As a child, I used to go into my closet and shut the door. It was dark and quiet in there—just the way I liked it. I'd push a shirt under the crack in the door to block out any remaining light, lay down, and pretend I was in the deepest, blackest part of the ocean. My arms would paddle the air, and I'd smile at the sinister and nightmarish looking creatures of the abyss. They didn't care that I was ugly, because so were they, and it didn't matter. They'd adapted to their environment, and it was wondrous to me, because I needed to learn how to adapt too. Being ugly above water means being lonely. That's just the way it is.

I was too skinny with a big head. Hair that was thin and scraggly hung from my head like limp spaghetti, a row of jagged teeth crowded my underbite, and my eyes were too far apart. To make matters worse, my mother stuffed me into the frilliest dresses imaginable and gathered my hair into half-hearted pigtails. Then she'd attach these ridiculous, colorful ribbons around them, not unlike those found on the handlebars of a child's bicycle. You can imagine how much unwanted attention that drew, but you don't have much say about anything when you're a kid. Did I mention my nose? It was disagreeable too, bulbous and wide on my face, like a blobfish. "Well, you didn't get that thing from me! It's just like your father's, your teeth too," my mother huffed once when I complained about it.

In third grade, I remember we had to do a project on where we would want to live if we could pick anywhere in the world. I chose the abyss, of course. I painted a diorama jet black, glued tons of the most interesting facts to it, and displayed my favorite book about the subject next to it. When we all walked around the room to look at each other's projects everyone laughed at mine and called it stupid. My teacher told my classmates to be nice, but then she took me aside, her hand gently nudging me to the back of the room, and she gave me the look of someone who was concerned.

First, she asked me why I didn't add any pictures to my diorama. I told her you weren't supposed to see anything, that it was the whole point. She had bent down in front of me then, her lovely face uncomfortably close to mine, and asked me why I would want to live somewhere so dark and scary. Her perfectly plucked eyebrows knit together, and she stared hard at me as I thought of a response. I still remember the look of pity and the smell of her breath as she sighed—peppermint gum and hazelnut coffee.

I told her I was A-OK and that the abyss was just where I know I would feel happiest. I'd had my arms crossed but pulled them apart and began to list the reasons why on my fingers. "First off," I said, "It's dark, it's silent, no one bothers you, it's unexplored, and best of all no one cares what anyone else looks like down there."

"Casey," she'd said, "it doesn't seem like a very happy place. The abyss would too lonely and probably icy cold, too."

"How would you know? You've never been. Plus, I don't mind being alone—or cold. Not everyone likes sunshine and rainbows. Ugly people prefer the dark." I'd crossed my arms again and stared back at her indignantly.

"Casey," she sighed, "You are not ugly. Don't say such terrible things about yourself. Look at these pretty ribbons; they look so nice in your pigtails. And your dresses are always so cute." A noise like a groaning dog escaped my mouth, and I rolled my tear-filled eyes, then stomped back to my seat without saying anything else.

Well, as you can imagine, that prompted a phone call home, and my mother went ballistic. She said I'd embarrassed her, and why didn't I do my project on New Mexico like we'd talked about. We went there sometimes to visit my grandmother, and she said one day we might move there so I ought to get to know it better. I told her New Mexico sucked big time and that I hated it, and then I told her I would rather live in a garbage dump than ever live in a place like New Mexico. After crying buckets and making a fuss, she did what she always did and blamed it on my absent father. She blamed everything on him.

I was sent to a counselor, but he didn't help much. He was young and my mother blushed whenever she came to pick me up and told me how handsome she thought he was, but I couldn't care less about how he looked. He hardly ever looked directly at me. In fact, most of the time he looked down at his notepad and tapped a fancy looking pen against it. He'd ask me stupid questions, scribble stuff down, then tell me to be happy with myself and focus on all the positives in my life. I snorted and told him I didn't have any.

One day, as I sat across from him, twiddling my thumbs, he took out a deck of cards and used them as a metaphor. He spread them out in front of me, pulled an ace of clubs out, and said, "We can't know what cards we're dealt in life, but we can try and find the ace in every situation." Again, I'd snorted and told him sometimes the ace is hardly worth anything. He stared down at his pad and tapped his pen.

To me, anything he said translated to "you're ugly, kid—just deal with it and move on, because life sucks and probably won't get any easier." But that's always easy for non-ugly people or even average looking people to say. In the end, the only thing I learned from him was to keep all of it to myself.

During mandatory holiday gatherings, even my relatives said little to me. It was as if they thought my ugliness would rub off on them if they engaged with me in any way. My cousins were all spoiled, and they liked to gang up on me like hungry buzzards on roadkill. This led to me usually going into whichever room had the least amount of people and sitting by myself, if I couldn't find a closet. I'd hear my mother crying and carrying on, saying she didn't know what to do with me and that I was just like my father. They'd rub her back and tell her it would be alright and that I was just being a little brat, feeling sorry for myself.

I grew to resent everyone, including myself. Bullying leaves marks. You might think when you grow up, they go away, but they don't. All those words sink in, layer by layer, until they're subterranean, entrenched and wrapped around your innards. You know how people who lose a limb still have pain where that limb was? It's just like that. The throbbing ache is always there, always with you.

Middle school was the worst, because that's where everyone's pushing and shoving to find their place in the ranks—conform or else! Except me. I knew my place, so I stayed still and let others use me like a stepladder. But I never fought back because they liked that. But I also never believed the whole rigamarole, "if you ignore them, they'll leave you alone." No, they don't. You fight back, and you're hit with rocks. You don't fight back, you're still hit with rocks. Those were the worst three years of my life.

In high school I was a ghost. People pretended they couldn't see me. I could float anywhere without having to ever utter a single word all day long. Instead of calling me names, I supposed my punishment was being shunned, so in a way, I guess they'd matured. I had one or two people who I might've called acquaintances, but really they just liked copying off my math tests. I didn't believe in friends. Friends were just people who hadn't screwed you over yet.

In my senior year I said the hell with it and did something I'd never done. For once, I decided to go to a school event. *Why should I be the only senior who missed their prom*, I'd thought. When my mother stopped laughing, she gave me money to buy a dress and even said I could borrow the car. I got a plain black gown that fit me alright and even got my hair done.

The day of, my mother stayed out of my way and drank vodka sodas like it was an open bar at a wedding. She didn't give me any advice or ask me any questions, and she never asked to see my dress. I got ready by myself and when I was satisfied with how I looked, I left my room and went to my mother's bathroom. I found what I was looking for right away and put it in my purse. I left quietly without saying goodbye. She was asleep in front of the television with a disposable camera in one hand and an empty glass in the other.

Our prom was at a hotel and was decorated to look like the Oscars, red carpet included. I walked down that carpet with my head down and once inside, floated unnoticed to the punch bowl. I sipped the red tropical punch and looked around at all the gorgeous girls in their exquisite dresses. A slow song came on and couples swayed together, and I swayed too, with my mouth resting against my cup instead of a shoulder. I gazed at them all with tears brimming my eyes and after a while, I did what I always do, and left to find a place to be alone.

The drive to the ocean took me about forty minutes. I parked the car across the street in front of two closed up beach shops, then I took my pumps off and jogged until my feet hit the cool, soft, sugar sand. The salty mist hit my face, and for the first time that night, I smiled. No one was around and the infinite ocean stared back at me, asking me what I wanted. She called to me, her voice booming through the crashing waves, over and over until I called back. "I want to be free." She answered me with a sighing whoosh.

I ran to the water's edge. It was cold as it lapped at my feet and soaked the bottom of my dress. I opened my purse and took the bottle of Xanax out. My mother had been popping them for years. I put one on my tongue and let it dissolve. The bitterness caused my saliva to gather. I put two more in. Then another and another and another and another...

Corpses don't sink. I hadn't been sure about that, but turns out, it didn't matter. I just hoped my foul and revolting skin suit would be consumed by something before anyone ever found it. I didn't need a body to go where I was going anyhow. I was a ghost again, but this time I chose to be. I have no idea how long I wandered above the rippling waves before I decided to go down. Days, weeks, months? I still don't know. One day I just stopped wandering and descended for what felt like an eternity.

I knew when I was there. My incandescent form drifted and lit up my surroundings in the inky blackness. I spread my long luminescent tendrils, splayed them out for all to see and pirouetted in pure delight. Jellyfish danced alongside me, along with a toothy grinning fish. I didn't need to hide ever again. I was home, and I was beautiful, mingling among the deep-sea creatures, where I would be forever. I had evolved.

Leviathan

Lucy Frost

*L*IFE IS A period of electrical tension in the flesh. Every cell in your body is a living thing, an individual organism; none of them are you—each is itself, a neighbor of its neighbors, partaking in no existence other than its own, but supporting its part of the community whose physical procedures are the platform of your selfhood—there are about thirty trillion of these cells, bound in the shape of your body—participating, *each for its own protection—traveling mindlessly down a biochemical path of least resistance*, in the corporate organization hewn from the indiscriminate probabilistic slaughter of nature by itself—the degradation of organic matter *towards* complexity rather than towards simplicity; in the sculpture by random explosion we call "evolution"—massed into a neighborhood of thirty trillion unconscious narcissists, knowing not even a wish to stay alive—in the blank electrical drive of a disposition pasted upon their form by the procedure that wrought them—*securing their prolonged existence for no reason other than the fact that they already exist*—clustering each for its own unmotivated protection into a contiguity thirty trillion times the size of any one of them; and in a shape whose contours work upon it, during a phase of its precise composition, the aspect of "consciousness"—a type of compounded self-directed receptivity whose functional basis inheres in no cell—and has no claim upon the use of those cells as media for its existence other than their obliviousness to it and its inability to perceive them except as grouped by their millions—this *thing*—"you"— "me"— "people"—ontological invaders of their own bodies; *aspects of aggregations*—patterns of current—habits of circuitry—existing nowhere and everywhere in the massed bunkers of single-celled life—echoes of energy reverberating through their fleshy course and dissipating—the facts of our living—an accumulation that thinks—and our world is an accumulation of *us*—and I see no way out of the idea that this *us* must also be capable of an abstract selfhood; but: as we exist at a level of complexity differing not only in degree but in kind from the complexity of any of our cells, so too would the *mind* of this high mass organism be of a nature abstracted beyond the functionality of the human mind, since its "cells" are people. If such a mind exists, that is, with only seven billion cells tentatively connected; but if the human population keeps increasing, and if technology keeps scaling up the degree of connectivity between them, this thinking, feeling Leviathan will presumably someday exist—if it doesn't already—and we will be as ignorant of it as our cells are of us—would be unable to conceptualize what that existence would be like, what it could possibly be experiencing or capable (or incapable) of doing—if it is, perhaps, suffering an extraordinary protracted agony (while we enjoy our lives—enjoy the individual thriving that necessarily brings about its existence and all its intractable pain—and not even know that we're doing it) and be powerless to kill itself.

Town Called Malice

Lindz McLeod

EVERY MONDAY MORNING, Kelly lowered her bare feet onto a plank studded with sharpened nails and stood up for as long as she could bear. As the metal tips sank into the tender flesh of her soles, she repressed a scream by biting her lip until the iron-red taste flooded her mouth. Thinking about the Before was a useful way of making herself feel bad, but physical pain cemented that mood, built it into armor. She'd once read a *Guardian* article positing the benefits of cursing as pain relief, so she denied herself the joy of even one muttered swear word, choosing instead to slump back onto her hard cot in silence. Bright pain chanted a rhythm with each beat of her pulse.

After two years, her memories were still reasonably fresh; each bleeding with familiarity like a wound repeatedly opened. Being scolded in front of colleagues for a minor mistake. A man's hand squeezing her forearm while music thudded through her veins, a voice in her ear alternating between negging and pleading for her number. Sometimes she added a new detail, something which had never happened, but which increased the shame or anger of the memory. Pleasant memories could be twisted too; the smell of roast coffee, accompanied by pumpkin spiced buns. The way her cat used to nose her to check if she was asleep or just pretending. Her mother's cheerful, tinny voice over Skype, blaring out an update on her latest venture. Everything she no longer had. The grief of loss could always be relied on.

Becoming numb to the pain meant becoming complacent. Ruaridh hadn't stuck with the government-advised routine. In the end, he'd yearned to be Taken, longed for the end of suffering. He didn't have the stomach for self-imposed misery. Few had, but she'd thought he could have tried a bit harder. If he'd really loved her, he would have done more. She thought about Ruaridh constantly. It was a useful way of making herself feel bad.

Crowds of Them milled hungrily around the streets of Edinburgh. Kelly shrugged on despair like a wet jacket, masking her scent, and dredged up an old resentment over a crush she'd had when she was a teenager. Today was her thirty-fifth birthday. Tomorrow marked the second anniversary since They had taken over. There was nothing good about this week, much like any other, and thinking about her past birthdays was a useful way of making herself feel bad. Safely ensconced in dull misery, she nodded to an old man who was sweeping out his corner shop with slow strokes. He ignored Kelly in favor of watching an elderly One, probably his wife, shamble back and forth on the pavement outside the shop. The One crooned to herself, something high-pitched and old-fashioned, and seemed perfectly content to traverse the same area of pavement, occasionally stopping to sniff the flowers for sale. Sometimes, some of Them would join the old One, cooing and sniffing, and acting as if they'd never had any greater pleasure in life than a limp petunia. On days when Kelly struggled to remember anything fresh and useful, hating Them was a useful way of making herself feel bad.

She took this route past the corner shop every Monday, and the old man had never once responded to her greeting, his blank blue eyes parsing out the space between Them. Denial of social bonds was probably a useful way of making himself feel bad. If she considered the situation logically, he was actually helping her stay alive. She didn't think about it. There was no room for warmth, and certainly no place for gratitude.

She carried a too-heavy pack of groceries home from the supermarket, feeling the cuts on her feet ooze with every step. When she returned to the shelter, it was overrun. She poked Them with a broom, ushering Them out like overgrown spiders. One lingered on the threshold, fingers dragging dreamily over smiling lips, looking as if she'd been caught in the middle of a beautiful daydream.

"Go on, sod off." Kelly smacked the stupid, grinning face with the end of the broom. The One's nose dripped blood; pale fingers crab-walked up to the trickle, came away red. The One examined their fingertips with all the satisfied delight of a new mother, mewling in joy, and a couple of Them wandered over to see what was bringing such happiness. Everything made Them so bloody cheerful. In the beginning, Kelly had lost her temper more than once; she'd come close to beating one of Them to death but, even on the edge of unconsciousness, the One had still gurgled with glee, enraptured by her newly-broken limbs.

Kelly pushed the One out and slammed the badly-fitting shed door, which rebounded instead of closing properly. The walls of the shed were pockmarked with bullet holes, which she hadn't patched because being warm made her feel contented. She ate a cold tin of peas, which she despised and had picked on purpose, because being well-fed made her feel satisfied. She wrote a few lines in her journal about her day and didn't use her imagination, because daydreaming made her feel fulfilled. She stuck to nouns and verbs. Functional words. To acknowledge color was to acknowledge beauty. Far too dangerous.

Her journal entries often puzzled over what she'd taken to calling the Ruaridh paradox; he hadn't loved her enough to be cruel to her, even when it was desperately required, and surely that meant he hadn't loved her at all. Watching his face evolve from abject misery to innocent happiness had been one of the worst moments of her life. He'd chosen to be happy without her rather than miserable with her. *Selfish bastard.* At first, she'd thought They would simply die out—after all, They rarely seemed to eat or take care of their human needs, but as the days wore on, she'd started to suspect that They got their jollies from simply existing to wind her up.

Nowadays, there seemed to be more of Them than ever before, and as far as she knew, there was no way of turning Them back. Even if she could, she wasn't sure she'd bother. Ruaridh had made his choice and so had the others; leaned into positivity, like there was nothing more to the world than a cheerful outlook. They couldn't even talk; she'd listened to them babble at each other in a strange, sing-song voice, but the words weren't real. The listeners would nod and smile and burble back when they got the chance, but nothing of substance was actually being said. Perhaps she wouldn't have minded so much, could have learned to live and let live, if she hadn't seen Them tear the throats out of others whose happy smiles had faltered for even a moment. Hard to maintain a sunny facade with a set of incisors in your jugular. Better to stick to what she knew. Misery, as it turned out, didn't really want company at all.

One evening, the sound of cursing drew her outside. Evidently, someone had missed the *Guardian* article. A woman writhed on the ground, a thick red line seeping through the knee of her jeans. A broken fence nearby was the likely culprit; the polite, pleasant thing to do was ask questions, so Kelly said nothing.

"Oi, you." The woman's face was angular, her accent sharp. "You got antiseptics? Booze?"

"Yeah."

"Are you gonna help me or what?"

She didn't want to, so she acquiesced. The shelter wasn't big enough for two, not with the kind of personal space Kelly liked to have, so this was perfectly uncomfortable. She passed over a bottle of antiseptic wash, which she knew from experience stung the most out of all the supermarket brands. When the woman had finished writhing in agony, her wound rinsed and dripping onto the stone floor of the shed, Kelly offered a tin of peas. She kept the sole spoon for herself.

"Looks bad. Must hurt like hell." Jealousy rose like the dawn. She'd never had a wound that bad. She'd never been looked after like this. *Peas without a spoon.* Ruaridh had been too caught up in his own shit to care about not caring about her.

"It does."

She poured them both a too-large measure of whiskey—the cheapest, dirtiest kind, which tasted of airport tarmac and smelled like a freshly painted fence. The woman ate in slow bites, her long hair dipping into the tin, coating the split ends in green mush. She scooped another handful out. "God, I hate peas."

"I hate your hair."

The stranger looked at Kelly's lip. "I hate your mole."

"Okay."

She didn't have enough blankets for two, so they lay close together. Kelly didn't like to share, so this was perfectly uncomfortable. Outside, the herds of Them milled in restless, buoyant droves.

The days passed. Sometimes she and the woman spoke too much, interrupted each other frequently, turned their backs when the other was talking; their subsequent exhaustion made them snap at each other over nothing. It worked well. Sometimes they ignored each other for days, the silence just as fraught as the arguments. Once, the woman had kissed her. Her kisses were completely different from Ruaridh's, who had always been too gentle, too kind. She nipped hard enough to draw blood.

Kelly pulled back. "I don't hate that."

"Oh. Sorry." The woman leaned in again, met her lips with all the tenderness of a long-lost lover. Kelly wondered who she was picturing. "Is that worse?"

Somehow, it was. "Yeah."

"Good."

Kelly washed in the canal, put on wet clothes. Winter drifted on the air. Dark puddles drowned autumn leaves. She handed a dripping sweater over to the woman, who hesitated, her fingers curling into the damp grass.

"Don't worry, it's not really clean."

"No, it's not that. Listen, I've been thinking. I don't think I hate your mole enough." The woman was looking off into the distance, her hand automatically going to the old wound on her knee. The freezing water dripped from the sweater into Kelly's shoes. She allowed it to happen.

"Then you better go." She let the sweater slide through her fingers onto the grass, landing with a muted plop in a patch of mud.

"What, like, permanently?"

"I don't care." Kelly shrugged. "Up to you."

The woman made no move to stand. "You never asked my name."

"You can stay here if you want. As long as you know I'll save myself first, if it comes down to it. As long as we're clear."

"I hate how selfish you are."

"Okay."

"I hate you for living."

Conversation always stung, that was the point. The stress of constantly walking such a fine line was enough to keep her off-balance. The woman would leave eventually, or get Taken, or die of natural causes. They were no better than minnows in the shallows, waiting to be beached when the tide retreated. She would have preferred to be alone and said so.

"Me too." The woman put her arms around Kelly and wept. "Can't we try? Can't we give things a chance? Just for once?"

They stayed, locked in each other's arms, far past the point of romance.

That evening, they chose a random One who'd become separated from the others—a young man with a crooked nose—and led him towards the canal. Kelly remembered the way Ruaridh had smiled at her, the way her heart had skipped a beat when the woman had brushed her hair back from her face one day. The One giggled, following her. She kept walking, maintaining a slow stream of memories, just enough to lead him but not enough to draw any wider attention. By the time they emerged on the embankment, she was drenched in sweat. "I need a second."

"Sack up, bitch." A flickered glance. *You're doing great.*

"You shouldn't swear." Her nails had stamped purple crescents into the palms of her hands. "I keep telling you-"

"That bloody *Guardian* article, I know." The woman rolled her eyes. "If you mention it one more time, I swear to all that is holy, I'm gonna stab in your sleep."

They descended the small stone stairs. The One's giggles rose into a shriek of laughter.

"Easy! That's far too much," Kelly snapped. "You're going to have a herd of them here in a minute. I thought we agreed-"

"Shut up."

They stripped and led the One into the shallow water; Kelly's teeth chattered uncontrollably.

"Is this worth it?" The woman's face was pale. She could see each vein standing out on her cheeks and temples. How easy it would be to open them, to bathe herself in her lover's blood. She would be safe for a year on that alone. "Every time you look at me, you're going to remember what we did." The unspoken question lingered: *do you love me?*

"I don't know." She was answering both questions. The woman understood. They frowned at each other and, interlacing their fingers over the One's head, pushed down hard.

CODED DREAMS: GENDER AND INFORMATION PROCESSING IN *THE GREAT GOD PAN*

Macy Harrison

If other worlds exist, then what do they look like? And who or what resides in them? During the nineteenth century, new discoveries in science and math implied that these were very legitimate questions for humanity to ask itself—and ask itself it did. Groups as disparate as theoretical mathematicians, spiritualist mediums, and fiction writers—and many more in between—pondered the possibility of other dimensions of existence and what that possibility meant for humanity. The universe was suddenly much larger, and, to many, much more frightening and chaotic, than it had ever before been conceived as being.

Not surprisingly, to the creators of weird fiction, the possibility of other dimensions posed an excellent opportunity to frighten their readers anew. Few of these ever created so disturbing a depiction of the universe as did Arthur Machen in his 1894 novella *The Great God Pan*. In Machen's story, there is another world hidden behind our own. Terrible things live in this other world, things about which Raymond, a scientist with a peculiar penchant for the occult, wishes to learn more. His reckless experiment allows ancient evil passage into our world in the form of the she-devil Helen Vaughan. This female destroyer is in many ways the granddaughter of a host of literary female mystics who sow destruction and discord throughout their environments.

The mystic female is a character with deep roots in nineteenth-century Western literature. These characters, including Maria Schweidler in Wilhelm Meinhold's *The Amber Witch* (1838) and Eustacia Vye in Thomas Hardy's *The Return of the Native* (1878), demonstrate uncanny attachments to the natural world. For Maria, this attachment allows her to uncover an amber vein which restores her family's lost wealth. Her attachment to nature—abundant, fertile, bearer of gifts—underlies her inherent goodness and naturalness and stands in opposition to civilized society as represented by the minister who charges her with witchcraft after she refuses his advances; like him, society is corrupt, wicked, and bent on destroying the innocent to its own petty ends. By contrast, Eustacia Vye's mystic qualities, which make her a "model goddess," also make her "not quite a model woman".[1] Her mysterious, sometimes almost magical, nature alienates her from society; she cannot conform to the norms of civilization—indeed, Hardy aligns her with uncivilized, pre-Roman Britain by describing her "Pagan eyes, full of nocturnal mysteries"[2]—and therefore sows confusion and discord throughout the small village of Egdon Heath. Order—namely, the marriage of Venn and Thomasin that is allowed to transpire only after the deaths of Eustacia and Wildeve—is restored with her destruction.

Maria and Eustacia, each occupying her separate end of the century, are but two examples of mystic females in literature, but they demonstrate how these characters tend to exist in extremes—they are either very good, and receive fruitful rewards, or they are unaccountably destructive, even wicked, and meet with tragic ends. These very different depictions of the female mystic reflect the mixed, often ambivalent reactions of nineteenth-century societies to the sudden popularity of spiritualism and the occult. In her study of female spiritualists and occultists, *The Trial of Women*, Diana Basham describes how female mystics could be seen as threats to the social order:

> Prophecy offers itself both as a threat and a challenge to existing laws and paradimes [sic] of reality; a threat because its existence indicates weakness in the existing law and the heightened anxiety that accompanies it, a challenge because it forces that law to consider what has been pushed outside it and thereby offers scope for re-absorption of its

---

[1] Thomas Hardy, *The Return of the Native* (New York: Barnes & Noble Classics, 2005), 71.
[2] Hardy, 71.

demonic energies by a transformation of law itself. Whether in seances, medical clinics of parliamentary lobby, the image of prophetic female discourse challenging the law to contain, control, interpret or fulfil it...remains essentially the same.³

Female mysticism is potentially dangerous, Basham argues, because of its transformative potential. It implies a system is at work in the universe over which only certain females can exercise control, and—most terrifying of all for patriarchal Victorian society—from which men are wholly excluded.

In *The Great God Pan*, this conflict between female and male power implicit in female mysticism is illustrated by the misogynistic destruction of Mary. Mary, the conduit through which Raymond hopes to see Pan, is chosen not because she displays the sort of preternaturalness seen in Maria and Eustacia, but because, friendless and dependent on Raymond, she is convenient. That being said, her unusual beauty and mysterious origin, not to mention her very name, Mary, the name of Christ's mother, with its connotations of female divinity, do fit a pattern of the mystic female; these qualities separate her from conventional society and, as with Maria and Eustacia, place her in grave danger by alienating her from sources of help. Whatever Mary's inherent mystical potential, it is irrelevant to Raymond. The embodiment of asceticism, he is "unmoved" by Mary's affection, and states, in the face of Clarke's concern, that he would not feel remorse "'even if the worst'" should happen to Mary during his experiment.⁴ He feels that, because he rescued her from the streets, he owns her; as he tells Clarke, "'her life is mine, to use as I see fit.'"⁵ No other reason is given for why he chooses Mary; though Clarke's reflection that Mary "was so beautiful that [he] did not wonder at what the doctor had written to him,"⁶ with its uncomfortably unanswered question of what exactly *had* the doctor written to him, suggests that Raymond may want to use her, not despite her beauty, but in spite of it. After all, isn't his proclaimed indifference towards Mary's safety rather suspect? Doesn't he insist a little too much that

---

³ Diana Basham, *The Trial of Women: Feminism and the Occult Sciences in Victorian Literature and Society* (New York: New York University Press, 1992), 51-52.
⁴ Arthur Machen, *The Great God Pan*. In *Classic Horror Stories* (New York: Barnes & Noble, Inc., 2015), 388; 391.
⁵ Machen, 388.
⁶ Machen, 391.

he doesn't care? When he makes sure that Clarke hears Mary say that she entrusts her safety to him, Raymond is attempting to deflect responsibility for her wellbeing away from himself; this act shows that, far from being indifferent, Raymond acknowledges that he does in fact have a responsibility to Mary—a responsibility that he does not simply disregard, but flagrantly violates.

If Raymond's actions up to this point are not suspect enough, then there is also the issue of the knife which he uses to operate on Mary's brain. This violent penetration is rife with Freudian imagery of sexual violence. When he describes how he knows exactly which "nerve-centers" to manipulate in order to see Pan,[7] his very language reflects the connection he sees between physical intimacy and violence: "With a *touch* I can bring them into play, with a *touch*, I say, I can set free the current, with a *touch* I can complete the communication between this world of sense and—we shall be able to finish the sentence later on. Yes, the *knife* is necessary; but think what that *knife* will effect."[8] The words *touch* and *knife* are not only emphasized by repetition, but are also stylistically linked by it. Physical intimacy progresses into violence in his speech just as it will in life when he kisses Mary before boring a hole into her skull and slicing at her brain with his knife. It is worth noticing also how he shifts from using the first person pronoun *I* when discussing his methods to using *we* when discussing how he and Clarke will interpret his results; by implying a shared responsibility with Clarke, he is once again deflecting full responsibility for the outcome of his experiment. A gothic destroyer much in the vein of Hugo's Frollo or Dickens's Tulkinghorn, Raymond seems to desire Mary's destruction more than anything because she is beautiful, and, being beautiful, she threatens his repressive, ascetic devotion to science.

Raymond expects Mary to be submissive and subservient to him and to his science. He expects her to be weak, easy to destroy and to discard. Yet, for all his preparations, he neglects her potential for mystic female (pro)creation. To nineteenth-century feminist writer Margaret Fuller, mysticism and motherhood are closely linked: "Mysticism, which may be defined as the brooding soul of the world, cannot fail of its oracular promise as to woman. 'The mother'— 'The mother of all things,' are expressions

---

[7] Machen, 388.
[8] Machen, 388. Emphasis added.

of thought which lead the mind towards this side of universal growth."[9] Women expand the universe literally by birthing new human beings and figuratively by mothering mystic prophecy. Mary's mystic insight leaves her impregnated not merely with otherworldly knowledge, but with an actual child fathered by a cosmic force. In a twisted mirroring of the Immaculate Conception, Mary's encounter with the spirit world impregnated her with a creature—a girl, not a boy like the male Christ child—a liminal being not-quite-human and not-quite-spirit, bent, not on saving mankind, but on corrupting and destroying it. This double mothering can be viewed as a synthesized expression of patriarchal society's fear of both female spiritual creation and of maternal creation. To Sandra Gilbert and Susan Gubar, male fear of female creation is closely linked to male fear of uncertain paternity, for, as they write, a "man cannot verify that his fatherhood by either sense or reason...that his child is *his* is in a sense a tale he tells himself to explain the infant's existence."[10]

The myth of paternity which Gilbert and Gubar describe, and which they present as a reason why male authors have tended to dominate literary scenes—for telling tales is a way to usurp female power by creating "an alternate, mirror universe" where they, men, hold full control[11]—has some interesting implications for the novella's construction. *The Great God Pan* is divided into seven sections, each with a different narrative perspective. Through these seven sections, the story unfolds in fragments—indeed, the novella's final section is called merely "The Fragments"—and half-told tales. Many occurrences are hinted at, but never explained or revealed, including Rachel's fate and how exactly Mrs. Beaumont drives her male suitors to suicide. If the telling of tales is a form of power, then *The Great God Pan* is testament to the failure of that power. Just as no man can explain or understand Helen, no tale can, either. To tell a tale is to define a narrative of events, and Helen simply defies definition. Her many aliases—Helen V./Mrs. Charles Herbert/Miss Raymond/Mrs. Beaumont/Mrs. Vaughan—imply an identity in a constant state of creation, destruction, and rebirth. Names, like categories, are adopted, cast off, blurred together, just as how

---

[9] Margaret Fuller, *Woman in the Nineteenth Century*, Facsimile ed. (Columbia: University of South Carolina Press, 1980), 90-93.
[10] Sandra M. Gilbert., and Susan Gubar, *The Madwoman in the Attic: The Woman Writer and the Nineteenth-Century Literary Imagination*, 2nd ed. (New Haven: Yale University Press, 2000), 5.
[11] Gilbert and Gubar, 5.

in her death throes boundaries collapse between categories such as male/female, human/animal, old/young. You cannot be defined if you are everything.

It is significant that much of the information the male characters accumulate about Helen is transmitted through the written word—newspaper clippings, letters, manuscripts, and inscriptions—rather than firsthand experience. Austin and Villiers amass a "pile of papers arranged and docketed as neatly as anything" in their effort to understand Helen;[12] though, interestingly, many of the accounts they collect are too horrifying for them to actually read: Austin, glancing over an account of Helen's doings, feels "sick at heart" and breaks out in a "cold sweat" before flinging the papers away unread.[13] It seems that the simple fact of possessing written evidence against Helen, even if it is unreadable, is enough to make the men feel confident in their endeavor to destroy her. And she must be destroyed—Helen, the indefinable, is an enigma and anathema to the male characters who must define, who must know.

Clarke's "Memoirs to prove the Existence of the Devil" can be seen as a metonymy for the male desire to define the indefinite, especially through the written word. By "reading, compiling, arranging, and rearranging" his accounts of strange and supernatural occurrences, an activity which is his "sole pleasure", Clarke is, rather contradictorily, attempting to catalogue that which is "unseen", that which is beyond normal, terrestrial understanding.[14] Importantly, he wants to *prove* the existence of the Devil—not disprove it. He likes to believe that the universe is full of strange and wondrous goings on; though it does not seem to occur to him that by cataloguing the inexplicable it will make it explicable, and it will no longer possess the mysterious quality which so intrigues him. It is also worth noting that in the title of his memoirs, all strange occurrences are equated to the Devil. Why is it the Devil, the great enemy of mankind, whose existence Clarke wishes to prove? Is Clarke's Devil the same being as Raymond's Pan? Machen never answers this latter question; to do so would be, as Clarke wishes to do, to collapse the uncanny distance between the known and unknown—a process which, as Clarke will learn, carries its own baggage.

---

[12] Machen, 419.
[13] Machen, 422.
[14] Machen, 392; 393.

As Freud tells us, the uncanny occurs when that which has been repressed returns.[15] Clarke is in the process of forgetting Mary—his renewed interest in the supernatural grows stronger as her face, "shuddering and convulsed with an unknowable terror, faded slowly from his memory"—when his young friend Villiers shows him a portrait of Mrs. Herbert which reawakens his memory of the "long lovely valley" where he witnessed Mary's destruction.[16] Though he realizes that the portrait is not of Mary, after all, the encounter leaves him shaken; however, his reaction is even more violent when he turns the portrait over and reads the inscription: *Helen*. While the portrait reawakens his memory, and unnerves him, the inscription fills him with such horror that he has a nervous attack and cannot speak for many minutes. Here again the reliance on the written word supersedes all other information, sensory or otherwise. Though some part of him instantly recognizes a connection between Helen Vaughan and Mary, it is not until he encounters written confirmation of his gut instinct that he truly believes what he has already intuited—that Helen is related to Mary, and that the consequences of Raymond's experiment are even direr that he previously thought.

The need of the male characters to impose a system of order—even if it be a system built on fragments and unreadable material—onto the strange and frightening events they encounter demonstrates their need to re-establish male power over the chaotic, supernatural female forces which have, to return to Basham, threatened the existing laws of society, nature, and religion. The religious dimension of *The Great God Pan* has been hinted at so far but has yet to be analyzed in depth. The implicit question of Clarke's manuscript "Memoirs to prove the Existence of the Devil" is evocative of the religious doubt which plagued Victorian society—for if the Devil cannot be said to exist, then can God be said, with any certainty, to exist, either? Any scholar of the nineteenth century will be familiar with how challenges to religious theory, notably from Darwinism and German critical analyses of the Bible, produced the opposing societal responses of total religious doubt and strengthened devotion through the Evangelical Movement. Somewhere between these two extremes appeared the Occult Revival and spiritualism. Howard Kerr explains how the spiritualist movement bridged the divide between religion and the new sciences:

---

[15] Sigmund Freud, *The Uncanny* (New York: Penguin Books, 2003), 147-150.
[16] Machen, 392; 407.

> The rise of [spiritualism] to such proportions was in part an extension into religious affairs of popular ideas of technological progress and 'scientific' miracle...For some believers, moreover, the spirit world was merely a newly discovered and higher stage of evolution, the spirit body a form of matter too ethereal for living men to perceive...The religious implication of this millennial impulse was that men no longer needed to depend on church and clergy and scripture for proof of the soul's immortality.[17]

Spiritualists and occultists proposed various theories about the mechanics of the afterlife; Kerr describes how some perceived the afterlife as being comprised of various "spheres" of existence through which the soul progressed on its journey to full development.[18] The influence of Darwinism can be seen in this scheme in which the soul, like material organisms, undergoes various stages of evolution in order to achieve its full potential.

A perhaps less well-known, but equally important, influence on spiritualist conceptions of the afterlife was the new mathematical philosophy of non-Euclidean geometry which appeared in the first half of the nineteenth century. The basic argument of non-Euclidean geometry is that Euclid's fifth postulate, which, to briefly paraphrase, states that a line cannot be drawn in parallel to two lines which intersect and that the sum of the angles of any given triangle is always 180°, cannot actually be proven within the confines of Euclid's system. This discovery led many to speculate that in a fourth dimension of space, parallel lines *just might* intersect, and a triangle's angles *just might* equal more or less that 180° (some hundred years later, American writer H. P. Lovecraft would find the idea of non-Euclidean geometry particularly frightening and would use it as the basis for some of his most terrifying stories). As Srdjan Smajić explains in his study of optics and occultism in Victorian literature, it was not long before spiritualists appropriated the idea of a fourth dimension of space and time, speculating that it "concealed not just something but *someone* from our sight, namely spirits."[19]

---

[17] Howard Kerr, *Mediums, and Spirit-Rappers, and Roaring Radicals: Spiritualism in American Literature, 1850-1900* (Champaign: University of Illinois Press, 1973), 9-11.
[18] Kerr, 10.
[19] Srdjan Smajić, *Ghost Seers, Detectives, and Spiritualists: Theories in Victorian Literature and Science* (Cambridge: Cambridge University Press, 2010), 167.

Coded Dreams: Gender and Information Processing in The Great God Pan

This sort of thinking has a direct influence on the mechanics of the universe Machen creates in *The Great God Pan*, as can be seen in Raymond's conception of *our* world and the *real* world hidden behind it:

> You see me standing here beside you, and hear my voice; but I tell you that all these things—yes, from that star that has just shone out in the sky to the solid ground beneath our feet—I say that all these are but dreams and shadows: the shadows that hide the real world from our eyes. There *is* a real world, but it is beyond this glamour and this vision, beyond these 'chases in Arras, dreams in a career,' beyond them all as beyond a veil...the ancients knew what lifting the veil means. They called it seeing the god the Pan.[20]

In this passage, Raymond's very language depicts a system where meaning is layered, partitioned off, and buried. Semicolons, colons, em-dashes, and quotation marks divide his speech in mimicry of the "veil" he envisions between the two states of existence; and the repetitions of the words and phrases *shadows, real world, beyond,* and *veil* suggest not merely dual plains of existence, but also that those dual worlds might in some way mirror one another. Is he not conceptualizing a version of the "alternate mirror-universe" Gilbert and Gubar describe, a "mirror-universe" spoken into existence in our world by the male tongue, an alternate reality which *he* can describe, and where the female voice, Mary's, will die forever on the mute tongue of senselessness? It is by no means a mere turn of a phrase to say that Raymond speaks this alternate reality into existence. Smajić, discussing popular responses to nineteenth-century German physicist Hermann van Helmholtz's assertion that humans, as three-dimensional beings, cannot possibly conceive of the fourth dimension, explains:

> Despite [Helmholtz's] warning about confusing the imaginable and the unimaginable, in popular culture the multi-world analogy operated as bonding agent between non-Euclidean and what are called *n*-dimensional geometries (of more than three dimensions), and spurred interest in considering ways to apprehend the fourth dimension. For who is to say what is or is not imaginable (*vorstellbar*)...to imagine something can also mean to speak about it in some fashion, to speculate on the nature

---

[20] Machen, 387.

and properties of a thing, without necessarily forming a mental image of it. In this regard, the fourth dimension...is very much imaginable.[21]

Quite early, the imagination appeared as a means with which to approach the fourth dimension; for the imagination is not bound to the physical restrictions of the material, three-dimensional body. Even contemporary popular physicist Brian Green invites his readers to "imagine" the endless possibilities suggested by a multi-verse theory of the universe and says that if "we let our imaginations run free, even the laws [of physics] can drastically differ from universe to universe."[22] Apparently, the human imagination has yet to conceive of a new way of conceptualizing other dimensions other than to self-reference itself.

To view the parallel universe which Raymond describes as purely created by his imagination opens up an entirely new dimension of terror in the novella, for it is horrifying to think that a mere man could, by the simple application of his imagination, allow such evil to be released into the world. But we need not even go this far to see that Raymond constructs a version of the alternate universe in his imagination, and that in his construction he places himself in a position of power; because he believes his imagined version of the other universe to be accurate, he therefore believes that he can control whatever or whomever this other universe contains.

Helen's arrival destroys Raymond's illusions of power and superiority. Like Eustacia Vye, she is an incarnation of paganism, the antithesis of male-centric Victorian society. Her name, unlike her mother's, is not taken from Christian mythology, but rather from Grecian. Helen, daughter of Zeus and Leda, wife of Menelaus and lover of Paris, is of course most famous for her role in the Trojan War. By naming the fruit of his experiment *Helen*, Raymond is designating her as a sower of discord—like her namesake, Helen of Troy, she will tempt men to their doom, and threaten to destabilize the social order.

It is not by any means insignificant that all but one of Helen's victims are male; furthermore, they all, like Lord Argentine, the first of the suicides, are society favorites, experts at "enjoying life."[23] The three suicide

---

[21] Smajić, 163-164.
[22] Brian Greene, *The Elegant Universe* (New York: Vintage Books, 2003), 366; 367.
[23] Machen, 413.

victims who follow Argentine are all "men of good position and ample means" who are "in love with the world."[24] From this, it can be determined that Helen has a particular victim type—prosperous men who, though they occupy potentially powerful social positions, choose to indulge in frivolous pastimes rather than engage in any worthwhile pursuits. They are men, in short, who do not take anything very seriously. The novella never explains precisely how Helen drives these men to suicide; what is important is not *why* they kill themselves but *that* they, men who love life, are driven to, or made to, sever themselves irrevocable from the world they love so dearly. It is a great reversal—and Helen is the epitome of reversals, dashed hopes, ruined fortunes, and frustrated expectations. The "entertainment" she provides to her "choicer guests", those men who seek only pleasure in the world, is far from pleasurable; it is a pageant of horror and death—it is an introduction to the "Great God Pan."[25]

Helen could be read not simply as an agent of destruction, but as an avenging spirit, punishing men who, like Raymond, spend their lives in selfish pursuits, oblivious to the suffering around them. Though these pleasure seekers are the antithesis of ascetic, goal-driven Raymond, they all approach the world with a certain detachment, a certain self-involvement that protects them from any "trouble or anxiety of any kind."[26] It is not a very wide gulf between *carefree* and *careless*.

While it may be over-interpreting to assign a moral motive to Helen's actions, she is nevertheless a definite social threat. She is upending the social order from both ends, working her way up from Trevor W., the son of a rural laborer, to Charles Herbert, who is "'country gentry'", to West End society men like Argentine.[27] Though each of these men is either killed, made destitute, or struck down by insanity, the social threat posed by Helen is not merely mortal; she also has the disturbing habit of moving in mixed company. A Piccadilly society favorite by day, by night, as Villiers discovers, she travels through the "meanest and most disreputable streets in Soho."[28] The strictness of class divisions in Victorian England cannot be overstated. As Judith Flanders describes in her excellent study of Victorian home life, every aspect of Victorian society was designed to promote

---

[24] Machen, 414.
[25] Machen, 422.
[26] Machen, 417.
[27] Machen, 394; 402.
[28] Machen, 420.

"social homogeneity" and "to keep the classes separate", because, for Victorians, "conformity to social norms was an outward indication of morality."[29] By traveling in social circles in both Piccadilly and Soho, Helen is subverting the social divisions which defined Victorian England. She is a threat not only mortal, but also moral—she exposes her victims to forces "'before which the souls of men must wither and die.'"[30] The corruption that is Helen Vaughan constitutes a death that is both mortal and spiritual; she oversees the complete destruction of her victims.

That she uses Raymond's name while slumming in Soho further indicates that revenge for her mother's death may be a motive for her destructive behavior. By using the alias *Miss Raymond* during her trips into the London slums, where she is well-known for "'nameless infamies'", she is degrading Raymond's name, associating it with crime, depravity, and poverty.[31] *Miss Raymond* is to Helen as Hyde is to Jekyll; it is an alter ego that allows her to shift between respectable society, on which she preys in secret, and disreputable society, where she can indulge her more natural inclinations towards destruction. That she associates Raymond's name with corruption indicates the disgust she has for him; or perhaps this is identification? For she, like Raymond, is breaching the veil and revealing the Great God Pan to mortal eyes. It is impossible to reach anything more than suppositions about Helen's motives, however, as she is never directly met on the pages of the story. Though she is the central character around which all the action revolves, she only appears in second-hand accounts. The male characters attempt to capture her in pictures, and written accounts, and news articles, but Helen herself remains a phantom made of paper. None of the male characters directly record their encounters with her, thus denying her a voice in their chronicles, and a chance to explain herself.

There is a certain male solidarity in the written word that comes through in the male characters' actions. They amass their papers to protect themselves, even applying judicious editing to protect each other's reputations, such as the censoring of the name of one of Helen's victims, a man who, as a "'respectable country gentleman'", does not deserve to have his

---

[29] Judith Flanders, *Inside the Victorian Home: A Portrait of Domestic Life in Victorian England*. (New York: W. W. Norton & Company, 2004), 24, 31.
[30] Machen, 422.
[31] Machen, 421.

family's name dragged through the dirt.[32] This omission of the name suggests that in the hands of men, information is arranged and edited, not necessarily in order to reveal the truth, but to portray a certain subjective, and perhaps even unreliable, version of the truth. Social and moral norms are coded into the construction of their language, norms that require that some names be censored, and some voices silenced. The idea that information must be coded for the safety of society is best voiced by Villiers:

> We know what happened to those who chanced to meet the Great God Pan, and those who are wise know that all symbols are symbols of something, not of nothing. It was, indeed, an exquisite symbol beneath which men long ago veiled their knowledge of the most awful, most secret forces which lie at the heart of all things...Such forces cannot be named, cannot be spoken, cannot be imagined except under a veil and symbol, a symbol to most of us appearing a quaint, poetic fancy, to some a foolish, silly tale.[33]

Villiers describes it almost as a duty of "men" to codify dangerous or forbidden knowledge so that only they, the cognoscenti, can understand it. Villiers, Austin, and Clarke are ingratiating themselves into an envisioned ancient secret society, much like the Masons but playing for much higher stakes, in which secrets that cannot be "named" or "spoken" are hidden behind "veil" and "symbol". They are but the latest initiates in a brotherhood formed "long ago". That this is a fraternal order is not questioned. There are no women among their ranks—women stand on the other side, with Pan. They are corrupted, like Mary and Rachel, or innately corrupt, like Mary's daughter.

Men in *The Great God Pan* are society's protectors—they locate the threat, Helen, and eliminate her—but they are also progenitors of repression. They repress all knowledge of Pan, hiding what little they actually know in a webwork of symbols and codes, and editing out information as they see fit. Though they are self-styled experts, the amassers of knowledge, when it comes to forbidden knowledge, they, like Austin who flings aside accounts of Helen's doings, cannot actually bring themselves to face the totality of the knowledge which they work to hide and to repress. One can, and must, compare them against the female characters

---

[32] Machen, 403.
[33] Machen, 422.

Mary and Helen who *do* see Pan, and who can cross the veil between worlds. It is their secrets that are being repressed. They, like Fuller's mystic mothers, expand mystic knowledge beyond the control of their male counterparts, and for that they must be silenced—they must be edited out.

Male codification results from male repression. Helen never would have existed if Raymond had performed his experiment on himself or Clarke, and his reason for not doing so is never explained. For whatever reason, they were unfit to see Pan, unlike their female companion. Raymond is furthermore unfit to deal with the results of his experiment; the child Helen is an "incarnate horror" for him—he cannot "bear" her presence, and so he sends her away, allowing her access to future victims.[34] Much like the editing out of names in the accounts of Helen, Raymond edits out Helen, ejecting her from his presence and, once again, refusing to take responsibility for his actions. Though male society ultimately regains control of Helen, they remain incapable of fully understanding her. That knowledge is sealed off from them. The inadequacy of their system of codes and symbols, of language, to process the information which those very systems attempt to obscure is exemplified by the Roman inscription which Clarke encounters near the village where Helen grew up; it reads "To the great god Nodens (the god of the Great Deep or Abyss), Flavius Senilis has erected this pillar on account of the marriage which he saw beneath the shade."[35] Though Clarke can surmise the event to which the inscription alludes, the antiquarians studying the inscription are "puzzled" and incapable of understanding it. The inscription begs the question: if only those who already know can understand it, then why erect it in the first place? The only logical explanation is that this inscription, like Clarke's manuscript, is another tale told by men in an effort to control, or to seem to control, forces which are in actuality entirely beyond their control and understanding. By deriving their power from codes, they are repressing the reality that they cannot actually control the forces that those codes represent. Their power is the power of letters and documents—the very powers which, as Basham describes, female mysticism threatens. By resurrecting that which has been destroyed in inscriptions and manuscripts, they are crafting monuments to their own inadequacy to understand the mystic female knowledge which they have thrust from

---

[34] Machen, 429.
[35] Machen, 428.

themselves, and so have lost irrevocably. Their codes are monuments of repression.

BIBLIOGRAPHY

Basham, Diana. *The Trial of Women: Feminism and the Occult Sciences in Victorian Literature and Society*. New York: New York University Press, 1992.

Flanders, Judith. *Inside the Victorian Home: A Portrait of Domestic Life in Victorian England*. New York: W. W. Norton & Company, 2004.

Fuller, Margaret. *Woman in the Nineteenth Century*. Facsimile ed., Columbia: University of South Carolina Press, 1980.

Freud, Sigmund. *The Uncanny*. New York: Penguin Books, 2003.

Gilbert, Sandra M., and Susan Gubar. *The Madwoman in the Attic: The Woman Writer and the Nineteenth-Century Literary Imagination*. 2nd ed. New Haven: Yale University Press, 2000.

Greene, Brian. *The Elegant Universe*. New York: Vintage Books, 2003.

Hardy, Thomas. *The Return of the Native*. New York: Barnes & Noble Classics, 2005.

Kerr, Howard. *Mediums, and Spirit-Rappers, and Roaring Radicals: Spiritualism in American Literature, 1850-1900*. Champaign: University of Illinois Press, 1973.

Machen, Arthur. *The Great God Pan*. In *Classic Horror Stories*, 386-429. New York: Barnes & Noble, Inc., 2015.

Smajić, Srdjan. *Ghost Seers, Detectives, and Spiritualists: Theories in Victorian Literature and Science*. Cambridge: Cambridge University Press, 2010.

Waiting for Golem

Alvaro Zinos-Amaro

Act I

The road to infinity. A pit stop.
Always evening.

HASAN: *(picking at scabs on his temples and on the back of his head. He studies the dried blood under his fingernails, then sniffs them.)* Curse this day.

KIM: *(shaking their head.)* There he goes again. Cursing this day, cursing that day. Why not curse *all* the days and be done with it?

HASAN: *(whenever Hasan is sarcastic, as now, he raises his eyebrows and smiles.)* In a hurry, my friend?

KIM: Just tell it to remove your pre-cap memories. *(speaking with aplomb now.)* Kill innocence; live free.

HASAN: *(speaking in an impression, but unclear as to whom he is imitating.)* How many times must I tell you, Kimmy, that this here little fella has burned through? (*his fingers tap at the side of his yarmulke-like cranial covering.*) Got as much control over it as I do the necrosis nibbling away at my big toe. Which, incidentally, seems to be rotting at the same rate as your memory.

KIM: (*self-pitying.*) Your cap blocks *your* pain. Every day the swelling in my ankles reminds me of my decrepitude.

HASAN: No cap in the world, Kimmy, could shield you from your burden. That emptiness deep within... (*paces, crosses his arms, looks out into the distance.*) It's the one thing about you that's pure. You're already hollowed out—so you'll never get capped. (*contemplative.*) A beautifully self-balancing arrangement.

KIM: (*sits down.*) I wouldn't mind trying to have a cap and failing.

HASAN: (*studying something only he can see.*) That's our mission statement, n'est-ce pas? Trying and failing.

KIM: No. We're failing and trying. (*their shoulders sink. their body eases forward into a slight lean of expectation.*) We're waiting for Golem.

HASAN: (*paces back to the starting point.*) What can that wretch do for us?

KIM: It needn't do anything. It merely need *be*.

HASAN: Look where merely being has gotten us.

KIM: The difference is, we can't change things. So, nobody cares whether we exist. (*they rub their hands in anticipation of a great insight, but lose enthusiasm partway, their arms falling limply by their side.*) I'm the okay that was, and you, Has, are the been that's left over. Understand? Me, K-I'm; you,

	Has-been. But if we meet Golem, they'll have to take us seriously. We'll stop being beneath contempt. We'll at least rise to greet it.
HASAN:	What's the difference? I've had tea with contempt, and lo, it turned out it wasn't my cup. (*speaking with great effort and measuring each word, as though wounded.*) Golem's not coming.
KIM:	You're wrong. You're wrong about everything, Has. Golem will come.
HASAN:	(*meek.*) Even if it does, what then?
KIM:	We'll use your cap. Curry favor with it. With Golem on our side, we'll be unstoppable. They'll have to acknowledge our voices.
HASAN:	(*makes a sound by comparison to which a scoff would be subtle.*) Basta così! Golem's not even here and already your plan is a shit carnival.
KIM:	(*impatience manifests as a repetitive patting of their belly.*) Your cap will love Golem. A transcendent handshake. They'll learn from each other.
HASAN:	(*waves his arms expansively.*) You don't comprehend the first thing about my cap. Since day uno, it's made me do terrible things and forced me to enjoy them. (*a flicker of the tongue.*) One time it puppeteered me into cutting off a frog's legs and then had me cry tears of joy that drowned its twitching, limbless body. (*icy grin.*) I don't choose anything anymore. Maybe I never did.
KIM:	I wouldn't mind a little fenta-nill right about now. Help me out. (*their voice mock operatic.*) Lancing my veins, what a cruel hypothermic needle this cold is.

HASAN: (*makes a sucking sound.*) Come closer then.

KIM: (*they raise their right hand, as though making a solemn promise.*) No. You only play with me. Nicks and nibbles. Licks and dribbles. No warmth—no way.

HASAN: Make up your mind, Kimmy. You want truth or heat?

KIM: (*pretending they have a cap.*) I was warm in my cage.

HASAN: (*claps.*) Very good. I'm impressed that you remember that far back.

KIM: (*clears their throat.*) The cage keeps changing size and shape, but it'll never leave me.

HASAN: (*picks up on Kim's throat-clearing, initially parodying it but then finding genuine phlegm and spitting it out.*) I'm jealous of those like you, selected for the cages. Les élues! You were right enough to deserve being wronged.

KIM: (*they rise, hold their right hand up to their face.*) I didn't do fuck-all. I didn't even figure out why they took me until years later. But somehow, *they* knew. More power to them, I suppose, for grasping me before I did.

HASAN: More power, less power, it's all the same. (*he tilts his head towards the ground.*) They're not listening. That's the point. They don't have to. Power is being unburdened from other's perceptions of whether you have it or not.

KIM: You once told me: "Die Stärke wächst im Geduldgarten."

HASAN: (*quiet, waiting for the inevitable.*)

KIM: How about a charity hit? Misery loves coventry.

HASAN: Here's something else I said: eating provokes the appetite.

KIM: Come on, Has. Just a little tweak. Whisper some sweet nothings about me to your cap. Turn that dial, let your nipples secrete what I need.

HASAN: (*stoic.*) The cap's wary of you, Kimmy. It knows you wouldn't be satisfied with one hit. And then we'd have a real sticky on our hands. Supply and demand. There's only so much it could force my body to produce. Let's not bugger Hippocrates.

KIM: (*feeling themselves winning a losing argument.*) You're hoarding that shit for yourself, Has-been. Hypocritical Oath if I ever heard one.

HASAN: What would you do after exhausting me and my supply?

KIM: (*evoking rain.*) What if I find us someone else to tap?

HASAN: My cap says, "Absolument pas."

KIM: (*convincing.*) I'll find someone. A kid. Healthy young body.

HASAN: (*eyes twinkling.*) Leave me alone.

KIM: Leave you alone? Now there's a notion! (*stammering.*) I could hammer-throw a freight drone into orbit with the force of that idea, weeeeee! It's not too late, you know. It's never too late for anyone to abandon anyone else. I'd do it, too. But I need you for Golem.

HASAN: (*chuckles.*) We're footloose, but our path is threadbare.

KIM: When I was in the womb, I dreamed of being here with you. Maybe I'm still there. O, sweet amniotic oblivion.

HASAN: My dear Kimmy. Whatever fantasy you thrive on, it always brings you back to this endocrine wasteland. Venice gone;

	the koalas choked to extinction. But at least we're on the right side of the wall.
KIM:	(*sing-song-y*.) Blood shaking my heart is what he said. Why do you never speak is what he thought.
HASAN:	(*patting his cap*.) They're ranting again. Maybe I should ask my cap to take me wherever Malone went. It would be better than this.
KIM:	If I'm such a bother, mute me.
HASAN:	(*yawns, but without contempt*.) We're both already mute, my friend. Silence can't be made quieter, except by sound.
KIM:	Let us be raucous, then!
HASAN:	(*takes a step back, no longer amused*.) You want us to rouse the world, is that it?
KIM:	(*negotiating a bargain, terms unclear*.) I can raise my voice, Has. You've seen me do it. I'm still here with you after all this time, right? Cheering you on? All I ask is that you feed me some of your juice. Perk me up. Ankles hurt. Elbows sore. Spirit sagging. Pissed myself again last night, and I didn't even mind because for a few minutes it kept me warm. (*they inhale deeply, trying to decide whether they wish the scent of urine were fainter or stronger*.) It all has to matter, or matter not, creating a choice.
HASAN:	(*pierced by the endless night beyond*.) You think Golem's going to care about your score-keeping? Your use of vitriol and baseness to balance the books?
KIM:	(*ecstatic*.) You believe me then! Golem will come! Golem will be here soon. We need wait only a short while longer.
HASAN:	They say, in unwitting mockery, that Golem doesn't speak.

KIM: (*on a roll now.*) Golem has outgrown language. He will know our thoughts with a mere glance in our direction. He will know our hearts with the darting apprehension of the places where our shadows fall. He will know our surfaces and our quintessences, and he will have the wisdom not to see where one ends and the other begins.

HASAN: (*mischievous, but also insecure.*) You're really hankering for one of my nipples, aren't you? You're practically drooling, Gott in Himmel.

KIM: (*not about to be trifled with.*) Golem will instruct. Golem will protect.

HASAN: (*now is the time to strike.*) How long did they keep you in that cage? Who else was there with you?

KIM: My brother and my sister. And the other nameless children. I s'ppose we are all nameless in the end. Our captivity took us back to the time before words.

HASAN: How long, Kimmy?

KIM: Kim, Sehr Kim. Simmered, not sautéed.

HASAN: (*fumbling search for non-existent pockets.*) Now we're getting somewhere. They put the heat on you until your yellow darkened to brown, didn't they? Turned your fear into feces.

KIM: (*bares their teeth; the gums are highly recessed and pockmarked with white pustules.*) It was a small cage, and there were so many of us, Has. We were gagging on each other's fumes. No room for agriculture. That was when I learned a valuable lesson: you can't harvest what you can't run away from.

HASAN: (*recalling a previous flyby near the truth.*) Keep going. My cap is nodding. It'll stay with you even when I can't follow.

KIM: They threatened us with poverty, but we knew it too well, so they threatened us with wealth. (*they massage their left earlobe, gaining speed, jerking the flap back and forth until the friction pulls off small strips of skin.*) Our cage weather grew obese, pregnant with expectation. Moon and tides anxious to see what shores we washed up on. Some of us disappeared into a perfect chemical mist. I don't blame them. But I could see what was happening.

HASAN: You didn't buy into the endless repetition of what they called night and day.

KIM: (*their old brown shoes kick a pebble lining the path into the void.*) A contradiction is a symbol representing the desire to dominate. I learned that in the cage. You embrace what you can't defeat; you win by opposing yourself. That was when I heard about Golem.

HASAN: Who told you?

KIM: The rumbling in my belly told me. (*snicker.*) The sky told me. The rain told me. The opening of the cage as they removed my brother and then my sister—each time those hinges creaked, they told me. I pressed my face against the chain-link fence, and the grilled impressions on my skin, they told me.

HASAN: (*moving his arms as though conducting a symphony.*) And then your turn came.

KIM: My turn never came. (*they try to count the stars in the firmament, but the attempt doesn't last long, as there are no stars here, only the echoes of starlight. when, they wonder, did they disappear? whither did they vanish? a conundrum for the ages.*)

                Before they came for me, the cage was opened, and we all escaped.

HASAN: Golem freed you.

KIM: Thirty-three years ago.

HASAN: *(meditating.)* Thirty-three years ago.

KIM: *(counting their blessings; a short list.)* Something about that night. We all felt it, divine intervention. My fingers grazed the bars on the way out, and at the entrance they touched little pieces of clay.

HASAN: But did you ever see it?

KIM: It was Golem. I felt free in a way I've never felt before. We were saved.

HASAN: Perhaps your parents—

KIM: *(their face lit by an invisible candle.)* My parents were dead by then. Mud on memory's boots, bones in melancholy's ossuary.

HASAN: What happened to the others?

KIM: *(inner wick flickers and inner flickering wicks.)* They made something of themselves, or they did not. They triumphed in war, or business, or love, or they did not. They lived, or they did not. And here I am, if I am. Behold me in my glory.

HASAN: *(releases the imaginary baton.)* And so, we wait.

KIM: And so, we wait.

Act II

Thirty-three years later.
Same place.

HASAN: (*holding his chin in his hand, eyes closed.*) The shortest distance between two points. You know this one, don't you?

KIM: Does my face look puffy? More bloated than usual?

HASAN: (*eyes still closed.*) The shortest distance is not a straight line.

KIM: Vision wavering. When I stand up too quickly, the world washes out.

HASAN: (*opens up his palms and holds them up to the heavens.*) The shortest distance doesn't involve folding space and time to bring the points together.

KIM: Skin itches. I'm always thirsty.

HASAN: (*opens eyes and clucks.*) No, the shortest distance between two points is found by erasing the points.

KIM: (*clawing at the bottom of their loosely fitting pants.*) Look at my ankles, Has.

HASAN: If we're one of the antipodes, and Golem is the other—

KIM: (*kneading invisible dough.*) For God's sakes, could you even wrap your fingers around one of my ankles? If you could, I'd let you stroke it. For as long as you like.

HASAN: I want to kiss you.

KIM: (*they raise one finger, then another.*) One, two, Golem's coming for you.

HASAN: If my cap were awake, it would enjoy the music you make.

KIM: (*in a lilting enunciation.*) Music is time catching its breath.

HASAN: Golem will breathe life into us—so you promised.

KIM: Golem will straighten us out, Has. Golem alone can fix things.

HASAN: (*snapping his head to attention.*) Did you hear that?

KIM: If you wave your arms and yell in a forest with no one else around, and a storm system develops three thousand miles away, how do you know you're not a butterfly?

HASAN: (*shivering as though kissed by snow.*) If I had wings, I would have fled long ago.

KIM: Seeking out the storm?

HASAN: I hear it again. Directionality distorted, meaning minced.

KIM: (*raspy.*) What does your cap feed on, besides you? Perhaps you stopped providing it sufficient sustenance, and so it slumbered. Spiritual anemia leading to phantasmagoria.

HASAN: (*a long-ago battle reclaims him for an instant, and when he returns, he carries still some of the sting of defeat.*) Don't talk to me about disfigurations. I'm the one who gifted you your precious dia-beauties, remember? You wanted to be insolent with insulin, you said, and now you're insolvent and incontinent.

KIM: It was fun while it blasted.

HASAN: Closer now. Even through the detritus of your indifference, you must be able to feel it. Air rippling.

KIM: (*as though imprecating.*) You're right, you're right! I felt grazed just now, brushed by the peacock of destiny.

HASAN: (*hops.*) It approaches!

KIM: (*skips.*) Golem is coming!

HASAN: Mon Dieu! At long last, at long last! (*wipes a tear.*) Cap is back! It was merely waiting for Golem's arrival!

KIM: (*rent by realization.*) Every particle beneath us is humming, can you feel it? Every molecule of the air around us dances with renewal!

HASAN: (*signals to a cluster of pixelated commotion, fast approaching them.*) There it is, Kimmy!

KIM: (*trying to stand still in place while the ground begins to shake.*) Let us dance and rejoice!

HASAN: (*takes a forward step and stumbles, falling on his knee.*) Ouch!

KIM: (*stretching out to pull him up.*) My friend, this is not the time—

HASAN: (*another convulsion sends Kim tumbling face forward into Hasan, who is pulled back down with him.*) You oaf!

KIM: (*crawling on all fours.*) I fall corrected! Perhaps now *is* the time, more than ever before! Let us bow before our providence! Let us kneel before our kismet!

HASAN: (*clenching his jaw.*) My teeth, my teeth! A shattering vibrato!

KIM: (*opens his mouth in an explosion of pus, as all the long-gestating sores on his gums pop simultaneously.*)

HASAN: (*averts his face but is struck by some of the pestilent debris. staggers sideways, begins to rise.*) Here comes Golem!

KIM: (*another massive structural convulsion, this one so strong that Kim is flung flat on their back. they yelp in pain.*)

HASAN: (*has keeled over and curled himself up into the fetal position.*) Our Savior!

(*stillness pervades all.*)

(*Golem towers before them, unmistakable but blurry, defying both visual and narrative magnification.*)

(*mute and inscrutable, blotting out the forever dusk with the memories of suns, Golem eclipses all expectations.*)

KIM: (*at last they drag themselves forward. their voice is a gurgle of toxic sludge flowing over sun-kilned rocks.*) Hail, Golem! My friend Has and I pledge our undying allegiance to you, o mighty hulk of all volition, o esteemed bulwark against awning darkness.

HASAN: (*spits out blood, along with several teeth. one leg surrealistically akimbo. groans.*) My tibia.

KIM: (*twists on the ground, pinned down by invisible forces. attempts to infuse his writhing with deference.*) We have waited so long for this. Go on, Has, don't be shy. Let us cap this misery.

HASAN: (*claws at his cap with his blood-besooted nails. laughs.*) No use, Kimmy. It's fried.

KIM: (*eyes glazing over with the delirium of ultimate disappointment. suffering becomes triumph.*) Your thoughts are once more purely yours? Tell me what that feels like.

HASAN: (*abducted.*) I'm self-shocked and shell-jocked. Too ashamed to swim ashore, too cowardly to drown.

KIM: (*surreptitiously craning their pained neck up towards Golem.*) A minor temporary setback, Golem, we assure you!

HASAN: (*debating who is more fictive, Kim or Golem.*) My dear Kimmy is right, kind Golem. You are not catching us at our best.

(*its gaze fixed on zero-space, Golem opens up its titanic jaws.*)

KIM: Has, maybe Golem is hungry? We must help Golem! It saddens me to see him so despondent.

HASAN: (*licking a fragment of sloughed-off skin.*) My cap could figure something out. But bereft of my one device, I'm left to my own devices, and have none to potentiate save magnificent impotence.

KIM: (*salivating, arms flailing.*) Perhaps those bushels over there.

HASAN: Too far. (*grimacing.*) But these clothes, I will gladly shed myself of them in order to help Golem. (*a breeze stirs; Golem, in its perfect immobility, reshapes it by dint of its mere presence.*) Here we go! (*with enormous effort, Hasan strips off his shabby black sweater and tosses it forward.*) A start, at any rate.

(*Golem is unresponsive.*)

KIM: (*moved by faith.*) And here are my brown shoes, o wise and merciful Golem. All these years struggling to remove them, and now they slipped right off my callused feet. Your bounty knows no limits.

(*Golem is unresponsive.*)

HASAN: (*tugs at his zipper; scrapes his skin, but eventually snakes out of his soiled pants; throws them into the mounting pile of ragged garbs.*) Feed on this for now, sublime Golem, and we will endeavor to secure a feast more deserving of your exalted being.

(*Golem is unresponsive.*)

KIM: My socks, my socks! How could I have forgotten? (*they peel them off and cast them into the mound of offerings.*)

(*Golem is unresponsive.*)

HASAN: (*heaving at the stench.*) My watch! It no longer marks the time, but it holds precious memories. Consider it a morsel of the past.

(*Golem is unresponsive.*)

KIM: (*they remove remaining garments; completely naked and goose-bumped now.*) Is this better, noble Golem? I have nothing more to offer.

(*Golem is unresponsive.*)

HASAN: (*doing the same.*) Please consume our humble tribute, gentle giant.

(*Golem is unresponsive.*)

KIM: (*shivering.*) And still he does not move. We must have offended him in some manner, Has. I would ask that you grab the rock nearest you and strike me a dozen times, wherever you wish, so that I may repent. Would this please you, o lofty and munificent Golem?

(*Golem is unresponsive.*)

HASAN: (*feverish from his broken tibia, forehead dewy with sweat while all feeling is lost in his toes.*) I have an even better idea; rip the cap from me, brother Kimmy. If Golem is silent, this is a sure sign that he wishes us to proceed.

(*Golem is unresponsive.*)

KIM: Very well. (*they inch towards Hasan; it takes a very long time, and blood and skin are left in their wake.*) This will hurt more than a bit. (*prying their fingers around the cap's insertion points and graft areas, digging into Hasan's flesh with nails, at last achieving traction.*) Does this please you, Golem?

(*Golem is unresponsive.*)

HASAN: (*howling.*) He who says naught must know all! Celestial mercy, o elegant creature of serene silence! (*a vastation of tears.*) Pull harder, Kimmy!

(*Golem is unresponsive.*)

KIM: (*knuckle-deep into the sutured regions, feeling part of his companion's skull melded to the cap begin to separate from the rest of the cranium; Hasan's brain becoming exposed along the side ridges.*) Accept this token sacrifice, o sagacious Golem of the ages!

(*with the massive trunk of its right arm Golem reaches down and lifts Kim up.*)

(*Kim lets go of Hasan.*)

(*in one smooth, uninterrupted swoop Golem raises Kim's jittering, ecstatic body towards its face and inserts the upper half within the chasm of its mouth and clamps it shut, severing Kim at the waist.*)

(*viscera arc down over Hasan, a rainbow of entrails and missed opportunities.*)

HASAN: *(outrage as a lifebuoy.)* Ah, well, if so you decree. An understandable sacrifice. Pray tell me, how did Kimmy displease you, o blessed and immortal Golem, that I may avoid his wrongdoings?

(Golem noshes on Kim's remnants.)

HASAN: *(reverence as a feeling of oneness with his surroundings and a subservience to the paradox of accepting his insignificance and its annulment of the very reverence which engenders its knowledge. also, blood seeps down his temples.)* I trust in your sempiternal enlightenment, o consecrated liberator of misfortune, and I know that you are incapable of doing wrong. I therefore offer up—

(Golem opens up its jaws and, as with Kim, consumes Hasan in two fell bites.)

(And for the first time in the history of Golem, something goes awry in the process of mastication and assimilation.)

(Golem belches.)

(The eructation is followed by a massive upchuck of Kim and Hasan's half-processed leftovers, disgorged with geyser force and sprayed upon the placid backdrop as a particulate crimson drizzle accompanied by a micro-meteorite shower of bone and gristle.)

(Golem shakes its head.)

(Stomps away.)

(Destination: the vastness of the continuum.)

(A few moments of nothingness pass, or do not.)

(And then a clutch of stars crystallizes overhead and winks softly at its newfound knowledge of the difference between the unpalatable and the indigestible.)

Straw World

Erik McHatton

HELLO THERE. WELCOME to Straw World, the most unique art installation you'll ever see! Right this way, right this way. Y'know, you're the first visitor we've had today. We're so glad you decided to drop in. You won't regret it. This is going to be mind-blowing. You'll see. I don't mean to oversell it, but after this, you'll think of life in terms of before and after. Ha! I can see you're a bit skeptical, who wouldn't be hearing something like that, especially given the hyperbolic age in which we live, but I'm telling you, by the end, you'll be amazed; absolutely gobsmacked. I promise. When I'm done showing you around this place, it will never leave you.

Straw World is the passion project of someone known only as The Artist. Pretentious sounding, I know. But what artist isn't at least a little pretentious? Tell me that. What they've—I say "they" because I've never actually met The Artist face to face, therefore I have no idea as to their specific personal attributes—done here is quite extraordinary but requires that we move through several different exhibits in order for you to be able to fully appreciate the experience. I understand this all may seem tedious, but if you give yourself over, the pieces will all fall into place in the end.

First, we go through the gate, the one there, at the end of the paddock. Do be sure to mind the rust. It'll be with you forever if you don't. I've made that mistake before.

Be sure to watch your step. The paddock is still in daily use. While Straw World does operate as a tourist attraction, there's not much money in it, sorry to say, so by day this is a dairy farm. See there, you almost stepped in a cow pie. You don't want that. The smell doesn't ever really go away, just stagnates. You know what I mean? It's one of those smells that you might not notice for hours or days at a time and then, BAM, it hits you when you least expect it. So, for the love of your sneakers, be careful.

Alright, we're coming up to the barn. The first stop. Now, you're going to think I'm crazy at first, that I'm far too enthusiastic for what appears to be a pedestrian display, but you just have to believe me. I know we don't know each other well, but for the duration I'm asking you to put such doubts aside. You have to learn how to appreciate Straw World. You have to ease in to get the full effect, like dipping into an extremely hot bath. I'll help you, hold your hand and ease you down, so to speak. I am your guide, after all. Okay? Now, if you look to your left, you'll see the first exhibit.

I know what it looks like. A row of scarecrow-like straw people dressed in old clothes, all shoveling hay. A bit hokey? Maybe. But look a bit closer. Look at the way The Artist has stuffed them, at the way the arms bulge, the legs ripple. Almost like real muscles, eternally taut, frozen mid-labor. Look at the form. Isn't that cool? The Artist is like one of those classical virtuosos who work in bronze or marble. A regular cow-paddy dodging Michelangelo. You don't seem all that impressed. Maybe I'm not doing a good enough job expressing it. Let me try again.

It's not just the astounding musculature or the realistic way the clothes hang. These straw people—all the straw people in Straw World for that matter—have the quality of personality, of life. If you were to think very hard about them you can smell their sweat, hear the grunts as they hurl the hay over their shoulders. Try it. Really think about it. See? What did I tell you? Looking at these hay hurlers now I bet you can see them more clearly; see the people The Artist put inside them. And you probably didn't even look into their eyes. Those aren't just tortoiseshell buttons, my friend. They're just like our eyes, windows to the soul.

Let's move on to the second exhibit, the straw children playing out back of the barn. The hay forkers are only meant to prime you up! These kids, though, this is where things start to come together. Just look at their buttons, how they almost vibrate with life. This entire diorama, and all seventy of its kids, were given the most meticulous attention. The beauty of it still takes my breath away. Here, walk through them with me. Just imagine some kids that you knew or know, maybe kids you once played with. Maybe kids you have. What does their play sound like? Concentrate on the memory of that play. Conjure it. Put them on the swings, in front of the kickball, and see if you can't feel them living, just a bit. Look at their straw faces and see if they start to resemble the children you know. Hah, they do, don't they? I knew you could do it. Not everyone gets this place, but I knew you would.

See those houses over there; blue, red, and yellow? That's where we're going next. The Artist really hit their stride when they built these. We'll start where they started, with the blue house. The "happy home."

Come on in, wipe your feet and let's go into the dining room. That's where the action is here. See? A dining room table, a family reposed at supper. Mother so happy her family is fed, father heading up the table. The children, a son and daughter, perfectly positioned, backs politely straight up and down, hands clasped together in their laps. The Artist even added the family dog, lurking under the table for scraps. Look at the hope in his buttons! It's those tiny details that sets Straw World apart. Seriously, sit down and take this in for a moment. Really let it inside you. Smell the air, I bet you can just sniff baking bread and broiled meat. Feel the hominess wash over you. Hard, isn't it? The Artist found it difficult too, even though their work is impeccable. Something about it just wasn't right. Families aren't like this anymore. In Straw World it's important to match the exhibits with the personal experience of the viewer (as much as that's possible, given the variety of people in the world), so a scene like this just doesn't connect. To most people this is a relic, held over from a time when we wanted this to be true. To some it's even insulting. It just doesn't fit.

The Artist began naming their exhibits with this one. They call it "The Lie."

On that note, let's move on to the red house.

The red house marks a shift in The Artist's goals for the artwork. There are more rooms to visit here, as the family of this house is separated, scattered like cast bones. We'll begin upstairs. First door on the right.

Move aside, let me squeeze in. This is the daughter's room—a profile of a teenager in peril. From the posters, the black bedspread, the scratched up photos stuck into the edges of the vanity mirror, one gets a sense of emotional neglect. Maybe you can relate in some way, or maybe you know someone. Picture the face of that relation twisted with the agony of being unseen, unheard, forgotten. Imagine their nights spent crying, screaming into pillows. How terrible it feels to have nothing and no one. Observe her carefully as she lies on the bed staring up at the ceiling, contemplating loneliness. Look at the pain in her buttons, the way the burlap stretches and shimmers around them, clearly marking the paths of drying tears. See how her muscles are almost all tight. How like a clenched fist she is.

Look closely at the nightstand. Do you see the straight razor? With just this implication one might conjure flashes of silver and red. Sprays upon the bed coverings. Slackness. One might pull the razor across themselves in their mind's eye, killing the poor girl through mental puppetry, just as you've just done. And when you killed her, did she look like anyone you love? Horrible to think about, I know. But you wouldn't be here if you didn't yearn for darkness, would you?

The Artist calls this one "Unspoken."

At the end of the hall is the son's room. "Assailing" is its title.

We'll have to open the closet to find him, sitting inside, his knees huddled up to his chest. Head against his legs, face obscured, he holds his hands over his ears to drown out indistinct shouting from another room. You know the type, the kind of pleading you might hear coming from a neighboring apartment, praying for deliverance from heavy blows. This is the nature of the son's sorrow. He is terrified, rage-filled, ashamed of his inability to stand and protect. He wets himself with tears. And urine. Smell that too, don't you? Ever know someone like this? Ever felt this helpless yourself? Who is this boy to you? Think of that person, let the feelings that brings up wash over you. Are you now fearful, angry, or ashamed? Or are you all three?

I told you this could be difficult.

C'mon, let's go to the parents' room.

Here, we'll just stand in the doorway. Okay, see the father at the end of the bed, the rippling tautness of his upraised arm, the flat palm about to strike. Look at the mother, cowered away from him on the floor, holding her arms defensively over her head. Can you hear his drunken shouting? Her whimpering? Have you ever known people like this? This man is that man. This woman that woman. This is where The Artist begins to ask for difficult things from Straw World's visitors. You *must* do as I ask for us to continue. It is no longer a suggestion or request. It becomes imperative from here on out that you put people you know into these exhibits, even if they don't exactly fit, and you must learn to carry out every implication in your mind. Strike the blow yourself. Let the sound of the slap reverberate inside you. Hurt as she hurts. Hear her cries for mercy. Allow him to continue on with none. Now turn away.

Allow yourself to feel the guilt of what you've just done.

This one's name is "Cascade."

Oh, and the family dog? Dead. Face blown off. Drunkenly shot for chewing on a prized slipper.

Which dog did you just think about?

This can be hard. I know. I'm sure you expected this to be a standard spookfest, but The Artist wanted this horror attraction to be much more visceral than any other. It must take a personal toll.

If you're ready, we'll move on to the yellow house.

The Artist built this house after growing weary of the blue and the red. You can ignore the sign on the door. The yellow sign, of course. I doubt you could make sense of it anyhow; I know I can't. I think it comes from some ancient language. The Artist loves old, dead languages. It speaks to their romantic side, I suspect. But romance has no place within the yellow house, so The Artist insists the sign is something else entirely. They say it gives the yellow house "horrible power." Maybe you've heard of such a thing, given your proclivity for horror stuff. Regardless, this is where The Artist's imagination really took off. Everything in Straw World outside of the yellow house is meant to be representative of the world that it mirrors. To those within the straw out here, it probably feels close to normal. But inside this place, Straw World takes a truer, more terrible form.

I know if I were a straw person, I would much rather sling hay all day, swing on the swings, or live in the blue or even the red house, but never in the yellow. And most certainly not in the black. But we'll get to that later.

Before you come inside, however, you must know that the air in there is quite heavy and smells a bit foul. It reminds me of dead pumpkins rotting in the fields. You know that dead vegetable smell? Well, this place always has that quality. I suppose it's because of all the death it contains. Don't worry, though. It's not the kind of death you're used to. This part can be extremely uncomfortable. Even more than what you've already seen. If you're squeamish you might want to stop now and go back. I wouldn't think any less of you, honestly. Plenty of people don't have the stomach for darkness such as this. Some don't want to be so directly involved.

You're still with me? Fantastic! Okay, try and ignore the smell and let's get inside.

Calling this one a house is a kind of misnomer, because, as you can see, it's just three large alcoves covered by heavy yellow curtains. You and I will go to each of these alcoves and perform a series of exercises designed to prepare you for the black, the big finale. Behind these curtains are experiments in horror, appalling straw sculptures completely unlike what you've already seen. The Artist has always had a taste for the macabre, but what they wrought here is otherworldly in its gruesomeness. Here, life and death are commingled in ways impossible in the natural world. You may think I'm overstating it, but in just a moment you'll see that I am not.

Before I pull this rope, remember, when this curtain opens, no matter what you see, you must do as I say. Everything hinges on your full participation. Anything less and we're just wasting our time. Alright? Good. Here we go.

This exhibit is called simply "The Mother." Look upon her prone body bent upward, as if offering herself to the heavens, her face contorted in something between agony and ecstasy, while her limbs, stretched in four extreme directions, are being ripped from her by black grasping hands emanating from the Void all around. Hear the sinews snap, the bones break as she's pulled to her limits. Her heart, still beating, *still* beating, exploded out onto her chest, sacrificed for those she cares for, her stomach distended, full and bulging at odd angles, forever holding its burdens within. Observe the way The Artist has captured the disparate torments of the mother figure. What a torturous thing it must be!

Look closer, carefully. Take your time.

You know what is next. You must now think of your mother and put her into this.

I do not know your mother, obviously, but whether you adore her or hate her (or something in between), this exhibit is designed to represent whatever she means to you. Perhaps it shows how desperately she sought to care for her young or perhaps it is meant to show remorse for the pain that she caused you. Hear your mother's cries now, as she pleads for absolution. Imagine the lagging beat of her dying heart as she gives everything for what she brought into the world. This is your mother. Repeat that to yourself and hold the image for a moment. She was ripped apart for you. Shredded. How does that make you feel? However it does, you must let it in.

I can see how upsetting this is for you.

When you're ready we'll move on to the next alcove. You might guess at what's inside.

"The Father."

Great, misshapen stones crush him, as his head and limbs protrude out from beneath. Bloated, painted purple, as if about to burst, you can see his eyes bugged out, ready to explode. The stones, shaped like people, are piled atop one another in a great melded mass of responsibility. Look how his lips protrude, open slightly as if about to speak. Perhaps to cry for mercy or perhaps for more stones. His fingers are splayed out, grasping, looking for purchase on anything that might ease this burdensome fate. But to each side of him—hammer to the right, nails to the left—the instruments for building are forever out of reach.

This is your father. You saw his face, and I didn't even have to prompt you.

Did he abandon you in some way or did he hold you tight? Were there long days when his absence was keenly felt as the hours slid by? Did you ever feel as if you weighted him? Which of these stones are you? How heavy was your hindrance? If you took up his hammer, would you place it in his hand or bash it against his head? Or would you instead lie beside him and accept some stones for yourself and be crushed by the same needs and expectations? Would you die slowly along with him as the stones pile high?

The next alcove is waiting. Take all the time you need.

This last one is the most personal of the three exhibits in the yellow house. I want to prepare you because this one is especially gruesome. It's called "The Child."

Behold.

Skinless, its inner straw exposed, "The Child" is stripped of identity. Those ribbons of flesh that have been torn away into tiny shreds from the bottoms of its feet all the way up its body— stretched from the top of its head and bowed out in the form of a cage around it—are the pieces of it taken off by those who were supposed to care. In their fumbling attempts to rear it, they instead peeled it every day. The yawning portal of its mouth moans with what has been done to it, calling out for its pieces to be put back. But even if one were to try, the strips of its skin would patch loosely together, overlapping, never properly healing. Look how it is splayed so like "The Mother" and "The Father," mimicking and beseeching its creators for providence. Look at the sorrow in its buttons, staring out of the bars of its straw-cage, knowing past wishing that it is forever trapped, never capable of flight. The air stings its exposed straw, cruelly.

Of course, this is you. You must put yourself inside the cage.

How were you failed? What are the causes of your soul's screaming? What cages you? Ask yourself these questions. Allow yourself to feel the unfairness of being born without consultation. Do this, truly, and you will be ready. Then, we will move on through that door to the right over there, onward into the black.

C'mon. Don't be afraid. Get in here with me.

Good. Now shut the door.

Welcome to the last exhibit: "The Black." The Artist's greatest work. I need to tell you now, this one requires a substantial shift in your perceptions of reality. So far, we've occupied something akin to reality, at least the reality you're used to, but "The Black" is about *actual* reality, and, if you'll forgive the pun, you're going to have to keep an open mind. Understood? Good.

Now the first thing you'll notice is that you can't see. There is nothing around us, and, as such, we exist in a sea of possibility. If not for the absolute surety you have that gravity holds you to the ground, you might float about, tumbling in the air. But lack of physical illumination is not the problem, it is lack of elucidation on my part. Right now, it is only you and me. If you need something to compare it to, think of how it must have been for you in the womb as you waited patiently for the world to open up to you like a burning eye. Think of this place as a vast, black Womb.

I apologize ahead of time for the subterfuge I'm about to reveal. Please believe me when I tell you the preceding theatrics were completely necessary. You see, this is not a story. I have not been speaking to some unknown character that you, the reader, have been half-occupying for the duration. If you were to go back and re-read the things I've said, you'll see that everything could have been addressed directly to you; was addressed to you. Now, considering these facts: I want you to try and re-contextualize the situation in which we find ourselves.

Are you still with me?

You might have made a few errors in your mental calculations, so I'd like to clear a few things up before we continue. While I am speaking to you from inside a written text, I am not a manifestation of the author's will. I am not the author speaking to you. I am a creature unto myself. An idea, born into the author's mind and pushed out into this "story." He dreamed me, and I taught him to create this place. Now, I've taught you.

My message to him, and to you, is simple. You and he and I exist in exactly the same way, we are all ideas carried around in someone's head. You probably have some idea of the author, even if this text is the only contact with them you've ever had. How strong of an idea, how clear the picture is, relies solely on the amount of information about them you've gathered. This is true for everything and everyone you've ever encountered. You see, there is something else you must understand before we can continue. It's a big one. It might be more than you can accept, but even if you don't believe what I'm about to say, just play along. Indulge me.

The universe is just data—an unending sea of information banging against itself, creating countless permutations of what could be: infinite impossibilities.

Allowing for this, what do you think you are? In case you still don't get it, I'll tell you.

We are merely possibilities, confluences, the endings of long series of events; eddies, rousted about by things of which we have no full conception. You are a drop in a boundless tide, unaware of what moon moves you. Do you know how your great-great grandfather met your great-great grandmother? Even if you do, there are incalculable other variables involved in your existence. There is no way for you to ever truly know yourself, much less anyone you've ever known or loved. We all exist inside of the mind. Whether it is the imperfect portrait you have of yourself—the closest to the real "you" anyone could hope to know—or the mind-puppets of you kept by others, you are never more than an idea.

So, that means that everything you know, or have known, only exists to you inside this place, inside of the nothingness of your mindscape, where the two of us are conversing right now.

Here, you are a god.

But you are not omnipotent. You need guidance to create; inspiration, data. To imagine a chair, you must have seen a chair. Go ahead, imagine one. Look! There it is, right on cue. Is it a familiar chair? Comfortable? The thing is, even if you try to defy me and create a new chair, one that you think doesn't look like any chair you've ever seen, you'll fail. You can only use external data to create amalgamations here. While the new chair might seem unique, it is still nothing more than an implication, made up of disparate parts of other chairs you've known.

Go on, sit down in your chair. Take a load off, for all that metaphorically matters, and think about how like the chair you are.

This all brings me to my point. As you may have already guessed, "The Artist," creator of Straw World, is really you, or at least you guided by me. The author and I created this place first, together, but its construction, like all "stories," is meant to force you to create it too, inside your mind. You see, if the universe is infinite, that means no matter where things exist, they are real, regardless of whether the information is within or without. So, everything we've created on our journey through Straw World now exists inside your mind, as it does for the author and anyone else who makes it this far.

Now, back to the mind-puppet I mentioned. This is the crux of it, the purpose for the entire endeavor. If everyone you know is in here with you at all times, ever-changing with each new thing you learn about them, shifting perceptually with each passing day, then that means you've spent this time placing very real copies of them inside the "exhibits" I described to you. It is your mother, the one you keep, that is being ripped apart. It is your father, crushed. It is you who will stand forever flayed inside your strip-skin cage, in here, in this pocket of creation you have wrought.

You just did it again. You see, your mind is as infinite a place as the universe, and everything you create in here is alive, not in any way you would understand or even be able to perceive it, but alive all the same. When you read any story where something horrible happens to the characters, you are doing it, you are the indifferent GOD that torments them for your own amusement.

You may dismiss all of this; you may think this is just the author trying to be clever. You might walk away and go tell someone about this story and how stupid you found it. "How pseudo-intellectual it all is," you may laugh. But we'll still be here. Even if you never read this again, we'll exist in the spaces between. Until your mind is gone, until you are erased, we will be. You'll think about this place from time to time, fleetingly, and you'll make another copy of it all again. You'll see the razor slice. You'll hear the cracking of your mother's bones.

Maybe you enjoy this slice of truth. Perhaps, in your hidden places, you like the idea of knowing that the suffering you can create actually exists. Perhaps you are the worst kind of sadist. Perhaps I've given you a great gift.

There is no way for me to know from my vantage point who or what you are. After all, I'm just a construct myself, with limitations all my own.

But I do exist, and I'll continue to exist as long as this "story" is out there. I'll multiply, procreating with each new reader to make more of me, and together we'll do as we've done today, sculpt the stringy stuff of the universe into this place. And when the last person to ever have heard of or read this is gone, then I will be gone, because in an infinite universe, the only law is impermanence. We all must eventually pass into The Void that waits on the other side of being.

So like straw; easily built, then blown away.

Wouldn't you agree?

Okay, now that my huffing and puffing is through, I'll leave you in whatever is left of the Straw World you live in. And no matter how long it is until we see each other again, remember, we're in here, all of us, the hay forkers, the playing children, the perfect family, the abusive cascade, your screaming mother, her rent limbs, your sputtering father, his bloated face about to burst, you, skinless, frozen in agonizing fear.

So, adios. Arrivederci. Au Revoir. Auf Wiedersehen. Goodbye.

See you again. Soon.

The Under Carnival

Logan Noble

NATHAN FIRST CAUGHT the scent of it as his taxi spat him out before his hotel. He raised his nose to the rancid summer air as the taxi rambled back down the road, returning to the interstate just out of sight. The scent, as the wind intensified, brought Nathan back to childhood. *There must be a carnival in town.* The air smelled like fried food and exhaust, popcorn, and sideshow games. Nathan inhaled it, his heavy travel bag and the suitcase at his feet temporarily forgotten. After the wind died down, the stagnant air returned, bringing Nathan back with it.

The hotel before him was a less-than-modest tower of cheap rooms and midwestern design. The nearest Michigan interstate led to this, shielded from sight by a sheer wall of elk and pine trees. Past the general grayness of the hotel and peeking out at its corners, lay more forest land. That's all Michigan was. Just more forest land with an occasional shattered city to break it up.

Nathan adjusted his glasses and picked up his bags. If he had time before his first meeting, he'd go find the fair. Was fair the right word? That's what they'd called them when he'd been a child. The state fair, the county fair. What was the difference between a fair and a carnival? He supposed it didn't matter all that much. The smell had brought out a sudden craving in him for the kind of food you could only purchase at one of these fairs/carnivals.

Maybe he could get a funnel cake and some lemonade? Some sugar and fat might be the perfect way to salvage what was turning into yet another massive waste of time. Nathan felt that so much of life was spent in places he had no interest in being in. There wasn't much choice involved. You woke up, you went to work, and then you came home. If your brain was right, you might have a hobby. Otherwise, you vegetated in front of whatever streaming giant had something new for you to consume. With his mind on the wander, Nathan dragged his baggage through the front door.

Lugging his suitcase into the air-conditioned hotel lobby was like stepping into another realm littered with utterly expendable hotel paintings and cheap wooden furniture that had seen a thousand careless bumps across their surfaces. Nathan traveled a lot for his job, staying in hotels just like this all over the country. He wasn't sure at what point all the hotel chains got together and picked out the wallpaper and the fake Ficus plants, but it must have been a productive meeting.

The clerk who manned the front desk was painfully plain. Because of this, Nathan couldn't help but stare. For starters, he was about three inches shorter than Nathan. His skin was milk pale, his eyes a ruddy brown. The clerk's hair was a faint auburn, slightly curly. Even his shirt and pants (the reliably dull polo and khaki combo) matched his general demeanor.

"Welcome, sir," the clerk said, his voice velvet soft. "What can I do for you today?"

Nathan set his travel bag aside and dug out his wallet. He opened it, looking past the credit cards and his outdated photos of Elise and the girls to find his ID. He slid it across the counter, Nathan's eyes drawn to the clerk's thin-lipped smile.

Something about the man was giving Nathan the creeps. He tried to push the thoughts away. It wasn't nice to think that way. The man was clearly kind and dull. *You don't know that. He could be a serial killer.* Dark thoughts. Dark thoughts he didn't need.

"Here is your room key. You are room 12, up on the second floor. Oh!" The clerk said, holding up one stunted finger, "That's right next to the ice machine! That's lucky!"

He handed the room key over to Nathan. "You should be all set. Please let the staff know if you need anything else. We are here to serve you."

Nathan dropped the key cards into his pocket. They felt slightly heavier than usual. It was clear that the hotel was seriously outdated. He could see it in the foundations of the building before he'd entered, in the slight fraying of the carpet at the edges of the room, in each ceiling corner dyed dark from decades of accumulated grime.

With the mild annoyance of checking in over, Nathan went to turn away and head to the elevators. That's when a thought struck him. Nathan looked back to the clerk, who was staring at him vacantly.

"Sorry. One other thing. When I pulled up, I thought I smelled popcorn and stuff. Like carnival smells." Nathan furrowed his brow. He suddenly felt silly. This little stretch of road was a pock-marked stretch of run-down hotels and a few grade-Z fast food places. As far as he knew, the area beyond this road was unreasonably rural.

But much to Nathan's surprise, the clerk began to nod his head.

"I'm glad you've noticed that! If you enjoy carnivals, this is the place to be!"

Nathan smiled. He had mentally prepared himself for two days of tedium with other accountants at the conference down the road. It looked like his infantile dream of lemonade and fried dough was coming to fruition. A carnival, even a local one, would improve his mood greatly.

"Where is this thing? Down the road a piece?"

The clerk shook his head. "No sir. It's actually here in the hotel."

Was that a joke? It didn't seem like it. The clerk's expression hadn't changed. He wore the same dead eyes and plastered-on grin.

"That's funny," Nathan said, scowling.

The clerk held up a pale hand. "You're misunderstanding me. The Under Carnival happens every night here at our hotel. It's happening under our feet as we speak!"

The clerk thrust a finger at the other side of the lobby. Nathan followed it. There, to his right, was a heavy metal door labeled **B**.

"If you think this kind of thing is going to work on me, you're sadly mistaken." Nathan could feel his face flushing red. He didn't like to be mocked. He hadn't liked it in grade school, and he certainly hadn't liked it in high school. And there was no way this *freak* in a tasteless red polo would pull him along on some kind of silly prank. "I'd like to speak to your manager."

The clerk's face didn't change. Nor did he pull back his finger. He kept it pointing toward the stairwell, his eyes unblinking. *Wait. He's serious.* Nathan could feel the anger draining from his body. He followed the point again, this time leaning backward to get a better look at the door. *Perhaps it's just a little carnival? A popcorn machine and a small, home-made game?*

Nathan suddenly felt bad. When he'd sniffed all those familiar smells, his brain had conjured a sprawling red tented carnival, complete with clowns and a Ferris wheel.

"Oh..." Nathan cleared his throat. "I see what you mean. I was confused for a second. I'm sorry."

The clerk's grin grew. "No need to apologize. Step right down! You'll love it!"

Nathan looked down at his bags. "Yes. I will. Thank you. I'll need to put my bags away though."

"Nonsense! Leave your bags here, and I will see they are delivered to your room."

Nathan nodded and walked away, muttering out a platitude as he went to the stairwell door.

It took him a moment to get the door open. It was much heavier than it appeared. He pulled a few times with one hand before switching over to two. Nathan grunted and pulled harder, feeling the muscles in his shoulders straining. The door squealed and finally swung open. With a grunt, Nathan thrust himself inside.

His eyes adjusted quickly to the darkness of the stairwell, picking up the weakly lit outline of a door at the bottom of the stairs. Nathan could once again sense those carnival smells, now stronger than before. The clerk's strange word choice came to him again. *The Under Carnival.* The meaning seemed clear. Under the hotel, under the clerk's feet. But it didn't make the phrase any less strange. With a sliver of fear in his chest, Nathan descended.

After the smell came the *sound.* The murmur of a crowd. That cursed circus music blared from blasted speakers in these gatherings from ocean to ocean. Nathan cocked his head and listened to the music closely. The light leaking from the door frame drew him forward, anchoring him. A draft had picked up, pressing low and then pushing past his ankles. A door handle floated in the darkness. It was deep-freezer cold to the touch. He pressed and swung into...

Outside. Nathan stumbled forward, his mind crashing into the new world before him. Minutes before, back up top, it had been dead summer and close to noon. Now, as a carnival uncoiled its colorful spine before him, Nathan saw that it was autumn and just past dusk.

He took it all in, his tear-filled eyes scanning from left to right, right to left. A Ferris wheel dominated the darkening horizon. Near him, crowds milled. Teenage girls in short shorts and half shirts. The teenage boys that followed after them. Parents with their young children, eyes glued to the ground. They weaved together in an amorphous spew of fabric and flesh, all different but all the same simultaneously.

The Under Carnival

Tents and trailers stood nearby, erect and busy. Strident music pumped out from unseen sources, omnipresent among the throngs. The murmur of the crowd rode with it, clapping Nathan on the ears as he stood there, dumbfounded.

Nathan swallowed. His throat was dirt-dry. He let his hand fall away from the door handle and slap limply to his side. He heard, though his back was turned, the heavy *thump* of the door finding its place.

He wandered further into the carnival, stopping only to read a massive wooden sign before him.

**THE UNDER CARNIVAL
GAMES FOOD FUN**

This place was somehow real. Though every fiber of his soul was resisting, that felt like a fact. Now he had a choice. He could either go back or push forward into this strange place. The wind gusted as he was slapped in the face by dirt. He spat at it and wheeled back toward the way he had come. Something was wrong here. This couldn't be—

The door was gone. Instead, far off, was a deep forest. Nathan could see the edge of gravel that marked the end of carnival ground.

Nathan wheeled around, panic lancing through his body. This time, standing beside the sign, was a familiar face. *The clerk.* He stood, the lights of the carnival at his back, his form a slice in the evening gloom. The short man leaned heavily on a blue hooked cane, a crooked red top hat perched above his ruddy cheeks. He wore a brown vest with a candy cane shirt beneath, the sleeves ending cleanly at the top of his pale hands.

The clerk dropped his mouth open and threw his free hand into the air. When he spoke, his voice echoed around them.

"Welcome to the Under Carnival! I am your carnival barker for your trip into the world between these tents! See the strong man! Taste the desperate flavors of our festival food! Step right up into wonders that no man should ever set his eyes upon!"

Carnival barker. Nathan felt that rage build up again. He felt his fists clench. *I'm going to break his jaw. I'm going to rip his teeth clean out of his head.* Nathan walked forward, his shoes crunching the gravel beneath his feet. He'd never felt so *angry* before. His brain was a storm cloud swirling with red mist and broken glass.

The Carnival Barker winked and lifted the tip of his cane from the ground. "To find your way home is just a short walk ahead!" The Carnival Barker took one long step to his right, finding a deep shadow cast by the carnival sign. As his shoe hit the dark, he simply *slid* into it, falling out of sight, a quick blur of red and white.

Nathan stopped in his tracks, all his hot anger draining away. He rushed forward, careening into that same thin shadow. Such a small space. Nathan fell to his knees, frantically searching the loose gravel. What did he hope to find? What was happening to him—a bizarre carnival, a plain clerk transfigured into an overzealous barker. There was no switch to find in the dirt, no easy explanation for what was happening here. Nathan was used to despair. It was his constant companion. But at least that despair had the decency to show up when he was comfortable at his desk or on the golf course. He had to face it: The Barker, in his bowtie and vest, was gone.

These events, as helpless and strange as they were, had to be addressed. He had to heed The Barker's words. His way home was just a short walk ahead. So, walk he would. At least until a saner solution came along.

The sounds of the carnival drifted over to him. Nathan followed them, his leaden feet dragging him along. Eventually, the dirt path that he'd started on began to narrow. The tents crowded tightly here, but the fabric was duller than before. Lines of people extended out from frilled entranceways, awaiting attractions that Nathan didn't care to imagine. Everything was graphically unreal, an organoleptic feast. All the sights and sounds greeted him, driving him further into their midst. A black flag rippled in the air. The sharp ring of a hunchbacked carnie driving in a tent spike. The blank faces of the crowds. The smell was exactly what he knew a carnival to smell like. Fried food and summer's end made scent.

He passed through the food area, scanning for a way out. He wished there was someone he could speak to. Nathan desperately needed to speak to someone of authority. There was comfort in authority. He'd been under its thumb for his entire life; sometimes that was easier than venturing out. He wanted to go back to the routine of accounting and his dull, gray hotel room. Unfortunately, there was no one. He was on his own.

The scenery changed, and Nathan found himself surrounded by rides. The metal deathtraps churned and spun, lights flashing and buzzers screaming. Nathan walked by one such ride, his eyes drawn up to the sign above it. There, in bright bubble letters, it read: **The Cardinal's Noose.** They all had names like this. **The Mother's Smother. La Bouche Qui S'Ouvre.**

The Demoralizer. Pale faces of the ride's occupants flashed by, each one completely devoid of emotion. *They're not enjoying themselves. No one is.*

Nathan pushed past the spectacle and noise, keeping his eyes peeled for a break in the chaos. The crowd pressed in around him, undulating as they moved, their teeth bared in laughter and sorrow. He'd seen the food, seen the rides. What came next?

The Barker awaited him on the other side of the crowd. He now stood well over six feet tall, his limbs starched white and stretched. His grin remained the same, displayed above a newly striped red and white body. The Barker raised one spindly arm. The voice that rang out from his mouth had grown deep and weighty.

"You've had your fun and your belly is practically *bursting* from all the wondrous foods of The Under Carnival!" The Barker threw back his head and cackled into the air. His performance, from the way his limbs twitched and the way his voice wavered, made Nathan feel sick. "Now you shall see the true wonders! A house of mirrors! See the oh-so unhappy clowns! Wonders that will make you squirm and scream!"

The Barker took one step forward. One of his too-small shoes sank wetly into the soft ground.

"What are you waiting for!? Time may be elastic here, but you still mustn't dawdle!" The Barker gave an extravagant bow. "The longer you remain, the less likely you are to leave."

Nathan shrank away from The Barker, fear turning his body cold. The Barker chuckled softly before straightening back out and striding off. He called back over his thin shoulder, his voice drifting on the heavy carnival air. "Tread carefully, friend…" With those final words, The Barker's slender shape vanished into the shadows.

Nathan exhaled. He hadn't even realized he'd been holding his breath.

Keep moving, he thought, once again forcing one foot out. One step at a time. The carnival area closed in again, though the atmosphere of this new part was vastly different. There was no music. There were fewer lights. Instead of the formless crowds, this area was largely empty. Only the sideshow attractions remained as loud and brass as before. Once again, his eyes tracked over them. **The Mirrored Death-March. The Nail-Driver's Show and Tell. SEE The Cubic Chair.** Standing among these tents, Nathan felt a new emotion wash over him. It was wonder laced with fear, astonishment watered down by fatigue. Whatever this place was, it was special. Why did he get drawn in?

Suddenly, from between two crooked displays, a line of clowns appeared. They were walking with their shoulders relaxed and their heads down. Nathan saw great patches of white and red paint on their sad faces. Their line came, impossibly long. He leaped out of the way as they went past him, dozens of men of all different heights, weights, and sizes. *They look familiar to me...* They wore oversized shirts embroidered with dots of color and great fluffed puffballs. Their trudge and body language revealed a great sorrow. It wasn't until nine or ten of them passed did Nathan realize why they looked so familiar.

They were his coworkers. Other accountants, just like him. He recognized Jaime Wents from the cubicle beside him. Stan from Cincinnati. His boss, Mr. Allen. Nathan couldn't contain himself. He rushed forward and grabbed Mr. Allen by his shoulders, shaking him. Allen's bald head, smudged with more of that pancake makeup, bobbed.

"Mr. Allen! It's Nathan! Can you hear me!?" Nathan continued to shake. Mr. Allen's eyes were vacant save for dark gems of sorrow hiding in his dilated irises. Nathan released his grip on his boss' shirt, and Mr. Allen fell back into line. Nathan watched them go, vertigo and faintness edging into his shrinking vision.

You're dead. You never landed. Your plane crashed mid-way through the flight, and this is some kind of limbo in those long moments before the darkness of death eats you up. Nathan thought all of that, his thoughts alight with dismay. Only his feet, ever faithful, drew him forward. Was this a cosmic punishment? Nathan tried to count all the sins of his life. There were too many to count. Too many to tabulate.

His thoughts directed him upward. Dizzying stars in so much black. What would he find if his feet could leave the ground and he could soar off into it? Cement? The unexplored depths of space? What did the cosmos look like contained within the floor of an aging hotel?

With the parade of clowns to his back, Nathan once again followed the path of the carnival. The attractions were all but absent now. The dense looking forest he'd first encountered upon his entry into The Under Carnival was closing in. An overhead light to his left flickered and dimmed. Was he nearing the end? It was starting to feel like it. Most of the carnival action was to his back. The path changed again, this time from dirt to sudden brick. It wasn't well-laid road; it was a mess of ancient-looking stones that the earth was on its way to reclaiming. Nathan squinted at them. Symbols had been carved into their surfaces, but they were not in any language or code that he'd ever seen. He did his best to avoid stepping on them. Something told him they meant something in this place. Walking on them felt akin to knocking over a gravestone.

The forest choked in, and the path came to its endpoint. This sylvan clearing's only item was a door. It was alone in the overgrown space, anchored to nothing and standing alone. The smell and oily air of the carnival were gone. They had been replaced by the earthy spoor of the forest. It was primordial, reeking of distant death and regrowth. But Nathan didn't care about any of that. His salvation had arrived by the reappearance of a stairwell door.

"You have done it. You have witnessed the splendor of The Under Carnival!"

From behind the door, The Barker unfolded. His transformation (if it could be called that, if that was in fact what was happening had taken a further branch into monstrosity. As The Barker straightened himself to his full height, Nathan involuntarily shuddered. One skeletal hand clenched the top of the door, his fingers curving down past the doorknob. His head (still humanoid, only twisted leveled out to the height of the trees. His body was bone-smooth but had been streaked through with the primary colors of The Under Carnival. His red top hat convulsed, seemingly alive in the dank light. He was double in size from when Nathan had seen him last, sheer horror from leering lips to tiny feet.

The Barker used his spindled body to motion toward the door. "The only thing that remains is for you to go through the door and back to your life. Your corporate position, your spreadsheets, and your swollen prostate." The Barker took a step closer to Nathan, brandishing his hooked blue cane. "Or... you can join the carnival! Live the life of a man tethered to a force and arrangement that you will never have the misfortune of encountering again."

Whispers were coming through the trees behind The Barker. They were not words Nathan knew. They were chimerical utterings, misshapen renditions of human speech.

"I am no thug. I will not lay a nail on you unless that is something you desire. The carnival is a vessel of choice; you have the power here. You will never be denied growth, never denied your deep-seated desires. It is forever autumn here, all-awakened dawn."

Nathan listened to the words. Internalized them. He knew he had no desire to remain within the carnival. He had no desire to become one of the faceless denizens of this twisted revelry. But was that true? The air held something he craved. It was a psychological attraction that had been present since he smelled this place on the summer wind. As Nathan walked to the door, The Barker's unnatural shadow enveloped him. The Barker leaned forward, his body fulcruming until The Barker's face was level with Nathan's own.

Was this a choice? It's didn't feel like it. What had he seen here? A carnival constructed to deliver a message? Was this some kind of lesson for him? Once again, it didn't seem like it.

His mind wandered to his life. His wife and kids, flashing teeth and displaying their summer discoveries. The paved driveway, the plain home. His identical khaki pants and his strangling suits. His desk with his carefully sorted pens and his stapler that he'd pathetically labeled with his name and desk number. He'd been there for nearly two decades, matching small talk and feigning interest. It was *his life*, organized and unspooling. All of those thoughts. But it was no riddle, no layered question.

In the end, the decision came easily.

Fugue

Joe Koch

THE EXPECTATION IN your grip transfers guilt like a nicotine patch. In the future, I won't regret leaving you. I'll wander with the rest of the amnesiacs not daring to catch a stranger's eye. We're buoyed by the collective murmuring under our breath. *Do you know me? Do you know me?*

Today, everyone in the world woke up with amnesia. Our driver's licenses and credit cards look like glitch art. We can't match faces to documents. We can't google ourselves without knowing names.

At first, each of us assumes we're the only one. We're reluctant to speak. If family photos once populated the shelves and walls, they've morphed into anthropomorphic abstractions, life-sized versions of Sims decor. Framed, the geometrical forms and blurred suggestions of teeth give no clue to who we are.

Assumptions upon waking. What else is there to go on?

I'm upset and disoriented by a false accusation in my dream. Someone at an old job said I was stealing. I feel angry, as if this happened in real life. I turn over in bed, and you're looking at me. I don't know how long you've been there or what kind of relationship we have.

The sheets smell like pomade and fabric softener. Light streams in through the blinds. We eye each other's t-shirts and disordered hair with hesitancy, paranoia.

You're holding a phone. Taking the cue, I reach for mine, or one I assume is mine. It's on the nightstand next to me.

The screen activates when I touch. No service. No apps run. You show me yours. The home screen identical, asemic.

I get out of bed. You follow.

In near silence, we explore. The bedroom closet houses extra blankets and a space heater. I'm awkward, in need of clothes. Down the hall adjoining a laundry room, there's a garment rack and chest of drawers. I don't want to take off my boxers and check the tag to find my size, so I pull down a random pair of chinos and slip them on. They fit. You grab gray jeans that happen to be the same size. Yours fit. Shoes, socks, ring; we're the same size, and everything fits.

We decide to leave the ring behind because there's only one.

Are we late? Neither of us knows. We discuss the next step. Do we drink coffee? Do we eat breakfast? In the kitchen, we meet two children. One huddles cross-legged on the floor, crying. The other circles in a bored playful dance, imitating the sound of crying, waving a wooden spoon.

You ask if they're hungry. You call out as if you know them, and for a moment I'm suspicious you do. The crying child hugs their knees and buries their face deeper in their arms. The playful one rockets away, squealing and smacking the walls with the wooden spoon.

You kneel down by the one who cries. They seesaw back and forth, covering their head, wailing over your entreaty. It's obvious you don't know more than me. I tell you to back off. There's no evidence the child is our responsibility. They may have wandered in from a neighbor's. They may be with scouts, selling magazine subscriptions, or be sleepover guests. Without more information, we don't have any right to make demands.

Reluctant, you agree. We proceed with our investigation, checking keyrings, notes on the fridge, mementos. Nothing sparks memory.

The television has no signal. The cable and internet are down.

The mailbox: we get the idea at the same time. If we're lucky, we'll find names.

The long gravel driveway leads us down a path secluded by woods. "We must be rich," you say.

I start to correct you and think better of it. We haven't discovered evidence to determine if we're a couple or a one night stand. If we're an assault, no mark betrays which of us is the aggressor and which the victim.

"This is a strange way to meet," you persist.

"We woke up together," I say. "One must presume we've already met."

The long driveway dead-ends at an empty country road. The mailbox has street numbers and no name. No mail today.

An old basset hound lounges in the middle of the road, unconcerned with traffic. We're deep in a rural town. A car creeps by, going wide around the dog. The driver peers out, nods, and slows.

"Gonna be a bad one," he says. The engine idles.

I say, "How do you know that?"

"Mm. Bit of rain later might help."

You say, "Always does."

He squints at the sky. "Nary a cloud, mind you."

"There's always a chance," you say.

"Yes," he answers. "That there is. Well, guess I better get on with it."

"Wait."

I'm not ashamed of the desperation in my voice or the urgency of my gesture. I grip the door, the open window, leaning in. "Where are you going?"

"Y'all need a ride?"

I yell this time. "Do you know where you're going?"

The driver cringes and gazes down the road. "That way."

"Do you know your name?" My voice breaks. My hands sweat on the hot body of the car. "Do you know us?"

The car engine makes an old oily sound like a grumbling stomach. The man doesn't remove his eyes from the horizon. "If y'all want a ride, hop in."

I dash for the passenger seat. You grab my arm. It's the first time we touch, unless we've touched before.

We must have touched before. We must have done much more than touch when we knew who we were, what we wanted, and how we fit together. You're a stranger now. This new first touch is a shock, an offense. I glare.

You cling to my arm unwanted and say, "The children."

I shake my arm hard, shove you, and take the ride to escape your guilt. Buoyed by the collective murmur under the crowd's breath, I wander the city ahead: *Do you know me? Do you know me?*

This Attraction Now Open Till Late

Kyla Lee Ward

"*H*AVE YOU SEEN anything strange tonight?" Madison asks Renato.

As they are both costumed for the House—Ren in his blood-spattered Victorian evening wear and she in the Housekeeper's gray dress and voluminous wig—there is an obvious comeback. But Ren doesn't make it. He lifts his gaze from his phone (they aren't meant to keep their phones on during shift, but all of them do) and says "You mean those two girls in the jumpsuits?"

"Yeah," says Madison, heart giving a little leap. "Those ones."

They had come through twice. Obviously twins, just as obviously under-age for this attraction, which only meant their parents had ignored the sign. More unusually, they were unaccompanied. Two little girls in matching pink jumpsuits who marched through, squealing at the jump scares and giggling in between. Madison remembers they had giggled at her, as she tried to keep the legend of Harrow House to a rating suitable for their tender ears.

"Little brats," pronounces Ren. "Did they touch anything?"

Madison shakes her head and then, very daringly, asks the real question. "What about their faces?"

"What about them?" Ren is twenty-four and has done television commercials and plays, as well as performing in the House. Under Lord Harrow's makeup, his skin is like raw, brown silk. He is very good-looking—it ties Madison's tongue into knots. "They were very pink," is all she manages to get out.

"Yeah, pink," he agrees. "Shiny, almost. Like they were made out of soap."

"Yeah," says Madison. Heart in her mouth, she waits, but Ren doesn't say any more. He looks back down at his phone and continues scrolling through auditions.

They are in the entry room; Renato, herself, and Noah, who is slumped in the wing chair on the other side of the fake fireplace, either hung-over or coming down hard. Although this is *her* room (the cast being spread throughout the House), they all migrate here during slow patches to sit in the chairs or on the lounge and take advantage of the almost-steady light from the electric candles—all except Selene, whose fantasy demands her own space. A sparsely-flocked fiberglass bear looms over them, beside a grandfather clock whose hands are set at five minutes to midnight. Red velvet drapes frame a portrait of the Harrow family in happier times, before the Lord brought the idol back from Peru. All this is normal.

The twins had not been normal, and there was something more. Something Madison hasn't and will not mention to Ren, or any of them. It seemed to her, as the two girls sat on the lounge where Ren sits now, that they noticed she only had one real hand.

Noah groans—a sound of pure agony—and slumps even deeper into his Beast costume. "Little monsters," he mumbles, and something that sounds like "some on four." She thinks she might ask what he means, only there is a knock at the door. The signal that more guests have arrived.

Ren gets up and hauls Noah out of his chair. The two of them stomp off up the corridor, into the haze of stage smoke. Madison quickly straightens both her posture and her dress, then at the last minute twitches her shawl down to cover the prosthetic resting in her lap. "Welcome," she says, as the door opens, "I am the Harrow's Housekeeper and have been for many years."

It goes no further, that night.

When the shift ends, close to eleven, they all trudge across the midway to the unobtrusive door beside the food concession and up the stairs to Wardrobe, to change and take off their makeup—all except Selene, again. She arrives at the Park in her makeup and fangs, and Madison has never seen her without them or wearing anything other than black. After that, the others go out through the car park, even though Ren is the only one who actually drives. But Madison likes to walk the entire length of the midway to the front gate now that the park is almost empty and there is no one to notice any part of her. The lights are all still on, electric rainbows looping from pot of gold to pot of gold. The fairy-floss and slushie machines are stained glass windows, throwing out patches of magenta and green, while above it all the Ferris wheel raises artificial stars into the blank night sky. Down by the entrance with its pastel portcullis and crenellations, the Twirly Bird spins like a firework in slow motion. Without people, it is beautiful. Even the crusting of rubbish, of popcorn cups and ice cream spoons, chip packets and discarded half-hot dogs, takes on a baroque grandeur, and Madison feels just a little like the accident never happened, as if she was here with a group of friends or on a silly, romantic evening (with someone who looks a little like Ren, in her fantasies), or even with her Mum and Dad. That both of them might be standing there in the entrance, waiting for her to catch up.

When she reaches the entrance, there is no one there. She trudges on up to the station and catches a train back to the apartment. When she gets home, her mother will already be asleep, and, when she wakes, her mother will be at work. It's better this way.

There is a knock at the door.

The new guests are ushered in and sit upon the lounge. Madison gives her spiel and sends them up the hallway, hears them gasp and giggle when the family portrait dissolves into the shimmering image of the idol. This distracts them from the first of the animatronics (the roaring trophy) which, triggering as they turn the corner, elicits screams. The House is all one, intricately-folded corridor; it is impossible to get lost, and you can run from entrance to exit in about thirty seconds, not that Noah had been supposed to do this, let alone record his times. Thump, a glassy crash, the tinkle of a harpsichord: they have reached Selene's corridor with the coffin and distorting mirror. Selene may get screams if they think she's just another dummy. From beyond, in Noah's room, comes scratching, the occasional howl and the thump-hiss of the second animatronic (the giant snake). But there's nowhere in the House you can't hear Ren, when he really gets going. His bellowed threat to offer their entrails to the idol, made while waving his machete in the final room, has sent more than one guest running back the way they came. But by now, the knock has sounded again, the front door is opening, and she has a new group to welcome and warn. Noah will have to take care of the malingerers, ushering them out the fire door. His fur and claws are supposed to be frightening, but children have been known to pat him.

On and on it goes, around and around, thump and tinkle, scream. Madison falls into the rhythm. It is almost relaxing, until the next guests arrive.

What is it about this couple? Madison keeps both the prosthetic and her real hand on her knees, not moving an inch, while the man grins, tickling his companion's ribs as she squeals and bats at him. Sculpted muscles and the kind of T-shirt that costs more than Madison makes in a week on the man; the woman professionally blonde and made-up, with inch-long orange nails.

"But when his wife and son were injured in a carriage accident, the temptation became too much. Lord Harrow wished upon the idol that both would recover and never suffer such hurt again." Madison keeps her gaze steady and her voice suitably sepulchral. But inwardly, she thinks his muscles are *too* cut, it's like they've been molded, and her face looks like it could drop off and crawl away... Madison isn't supposed to think like that. According to her psychologist, that kind of negativity only reinforces her sense of alienation.

She straightens up and, although smiling is inappropriate, makes a renewed effort to meet the woman's eyes. Then her heart skips and her tongue knots when she realizes neither of them are looking at her face as she speaks. They are looking, indisputably, at her prosthetic hand.

She stops in the middle of a sentence and, with her real hand, gestures for them to proceed down the hallway. They do, whispering and giggling, and she watches them. As they turn the corner, as the smoke envelops them, she could swear she sees the woman bring her date's finger to her mouth and bite down. She could swear that the finger comes off.

There is a knock at the door. For a moment, Madison does not, cannot, move.

Then she flicks the shawl down again and finds the opening phrase somewhere in her throat. As the next guests file in, hooting and mock-screaming, she does not look at them.

"No, they didn't touch anything." Madison can hardly get the words out. "They didn't threaten me. They just..."

"They didn't need to," says Selene, who has just emerged from the smoke. "It's their eyes."

Madison has never had much to do with Selene, despite her being the only other woman in the House. Now, she gazes up at her—straight, black hair, gray eyes, paper-white skin, and wearing the corset again instead of her costume. Madison gazes as if Selene is the sister she never had. "Their eyes," she echoes, "Like, you think they might be fake but then they *move*."

"Contact lenses," suggests Ren. "There could be a birthday party in the Park, and it's a joke."

"Sometimes it's their whole faces," Selene insists. "Sometimes just their hands."

Madison stiffens, but none of them look at her. She can feel them not looking at her.

"So, someone did touch you?" Ren glances at the corset.

Selene's eyes go cold. "They don't need to," she repeats, then seats herself neatly on the arm of the wing chair where Noah has once again collapsed.

"I'm just trying to understand." Ren pushes back his black curls (glorious hair, the kind you just want to run your fingers through) and looks frustrated. "What's actually the problem here? If they don't touch you, and they don't make threats or sex jokes—"

"You're telling me," Selene cuts in, "that you haven't noticed a single, strange thing?"

You have, Madison holds her breath. *You noticed the twins.* For just an instant their eyes meet.

Then he turns to Noah. "What about you? Seen anyone with weird eyes or han—faces?"

Inside their plastic shell, Madison's missing fingers prickle and twitch. They itch for the touch of curls, to flex and to hold. Noah looks sick, really, like he might throw up on the carpet.

"People are just assholes," he says, "Right?" But to Madison, it sounds like he's seeking reassurance.

"Right," says Ren. He uncrosses his feet. "Look, I'm not saying we don't get people through who behave like dicks. But if they're not breaking the rules, then what can we do? People pay to come through, and if that's 'cause they want to laugh at the freaks, then so what?"

There is a knock at the door. As though he was the one who had been laughed at all along, Ren slams his top hat onto his curls and storms up the hallway, before any of them can say a word.

When Madison gets home, her mother is asleep. The white-dark apartment is quiet and still feels both too small and emptier than it should.

She concluded regular appointments with her psychologist three months ago (two years after the accident), but she still has the number. She is entitled, they said, to call in an emergency. Is this an emergency?

Her missing fingers ache as she undoes the straps and slips her wrist from the sheath. She has learned to write passably with her left hand, but her brain has still not adjusted to the loss of the right. The doctors said it might take years before she stops feeling these phantom sensations, a refraction of the moment she did *not* feel, when the displaced metal of the car engine crushed her hand beyond repair. That was not all it did. She wonders if her sleeping mother sometimes feels an itch or prickle when she rolls into that half of the bed where Madison's father used to be.

What she is seeing now, in the House, must be something like that. A phantom. A displacement. Even if Selene agrees, even if Noah is spooked by something beyond his regular intake of recreational drugs, Ren is undoubtedly right.

The next afternoon, Madison arrives early at the Park. She does this sometimes, so as to avoid the crush in Wardrobe at the shift change, when all the clowns exchange their baggy pants and makeup for jeans and T-shirts, as the new batch pull on their wigs and oversized shoes.

Having become the Housekeeper, she takes the keys from the office and opens up the House. She turns on the power at the switchboard, which is behind the bear. She sets the soundtrack playing, looping through its tolling bells, moaning wind and scritching violin. She turns on the full, overhead lights (distinct from the effects lighting) and walks the entire length of the corridor, checking that the animatronics are working and topping the smoke machines up with smoke juice. She enjoys doing these things, so long as there is no one watching. It was how her mother got her to go for the job in the first place, by telling her no one would pay any attention to her here and, if they did, they wouldn't be able to tell a real injury from a fake one. Right, Mum.

But when she turns the corner into Selene's room, she sees Noah lying full-length in the coffin. He is dressed in clothes she hasn't seen before: a silver, sleeveless top with an inbuilt hood and pants that would be clown-like except they are black and supplied with an array of studs, eyelets and lacing. His jacket is hooked over the mirror. His chest moves slowly, evenly, and a slight sheen of drool marks the satin pillow. He looks, for all the world, like he has been here all night.

How has this happened? He left with the rest of them. Obviously, she needs to wake him before anyone else shows up, but how to go about it? Just looking at his relaxed, freckly face makes her feel embarrassed.

The answer is simple. She steps round the corner and triggers the snake.

Noah shrieks himself awake, trying to get to his feet, to get out of the coffin, and failing spectacularly. "Fuck!"

"Are... are you alright?"

He stares, as though her presence here is inconceivable. Then he says, "Yeah, thanks."

She offers him her water bottle, and he takes it, swigs half. Then he climbs out and disappears briefly through the fire door, for a purpose she doesn't want to overhear.

She is in the entry room when he finally sidles back in. Sits down. "You know how there's that big crack in the wall, right next to the fire door?" He says at last. "Well, last night I got the whole board out and climbed through. I've shoved it back: no one will know."

"Yes," she says, "But why...?"

"I came back here when I couldn't get home after the club."

"Were the trains out?"

Noah shakes his head. "I never even made it to the station." He pauses. When he looks at her, he is sick again. "It was the monsters. Some have two legs, but some have four."

She looks for signs he is joking. But he's not joking and actually seems less medicated than usual.

"It's crazy," he says. "I know. Unless you're seeing the same things, but then I..." He trails off, and his chin sinks to his chest. "Sorry. I should have backed you up."

"It's okay," says Madison, even though she feels anything but. His acknowledgement that something is wrong, on top of Selene's, is like a weight sinking in her stomach. "But you see them outside the House..." Of *course* he does! To come inside, they have to be outside; she tries another tack. "How long have you been seeing them?"

"Dunno. Since summer, maybe?" Has he had this fear in his eyes since then? "But there's more of them now."

"And they were at the club?"

Noah shudders. "The worst ones, they stay outside, and I only see them in the dark. But the one that can pass for human... don't *you* see them, like at the station or the shops?"

Madison shakes her head. But then, she actively tries to avoid people, except in the House. "We should watch today," she says. "You, me, and Selene. When they come in, I'll give a signal; trigger the portrait twice, maybe. Then we'll see if we see the same things in the same people. And you can check if you recognize any of them."

"Yeah," he says, "That's good thinking." He doesn't look much better, but he probably needs to eat.

"You should go get breakfast and then change." She stands up. "I'll talk to Selene when she gets here."

"Yeah," he says. "Yeah. That's..."

"I won't tell her you were in her coffin."

They pass through the House, those non-humans, noticing what they should not. That a young man has piercings and scars, more scars than he should. That under her makeup, a Goth girl is older than you'd think. Some of them look like adults in their prime, some are middle-aged, some are the size of children. Eyes that reflect, hands that extrude, some that seem to shed body parts behind them. These dissolve into a slime that might otherwise be mistaken for spilled soda or fairy floss. They come in the daylight, but there are more of them after dark. At the end of shift, Madison, Noah and Selene add up their tally (only counting sightings where they all agree) and estimate that a quarter of their guests are now monsters.

So, what is going on? For Selene, it started after she broke up with her last boyfriend. "It was like he changed overnight. I mean, that's what it was like for me. One day, he just didn't want to do our thing anymore. I hadn't noticed him changing, so I started trying to see all the things I'd missed."

Noah agrees with her, that they were most likely there all along. Madison is not so sure. They must have come from somewhere, like pollution or plagues of insects. Something must have happened. "An accident," she says.

"Well, whatever it was," says Noah, "They're here. What do we do?"

"I think we should watch Ren," says Selene, catching her black lip on a fang. "He can't see them. What if he's turning into one?"

Madison starts to say they've no reason to think that, except of course, Selene does. "Ren's alright," she says instead. "A bit stuck up."

"A *bit*," says Noah, and laughs. They all laugh and yes, it feels good.

"I'm going to look for something that could have caused this," says Madison. "In the meantime, I guess we carry on like normal. But none of us should be out on the streets at night."

There are wars happening that she didn't even know about in countries she didn't know existed. The weather isn't behaving like it should, with temperatures going up and down further than they ever have before. Lights have appeared in the sky, and super moons, and a partial solar eclipse.

That night, when she arrives home, Madison finds her mother sitting up in front of the shopping channel, drink in hand. She sits down beside her and, after a few minutes of watching the changing patterns on the screen, she asks when all this strangeness started, whether her mother remembers when *before* became *now*.

Her mother snorts. "There was no before."

There was. She remembers it. It was when she had a boyfriend (though it wasn't really serious) and was going to go to university and... what had she been going to do? Maybe study journalism. Maybe act.

Her mother falls asleep as a presenter offers to sell them small statuettes of something she can't quite make out. But Madison can't sleep, in her bed or anywhere. She ends up back online, doing more research. And when she goes into work (a full two hours early, this time), both Noah and Selene are already there. Signs are that Selene took the coffin and Noah the lounge. One of the red drapes has been brought down and used as blanket.

"I couldn't even get near my house," Selene says, voice stretched high and thin. "The police had cordoned off the road. If they were police."

Selene's hair is mussed, and her makeup rubbed away in places. Madison asks what she did then. Selene says she remembered Madison's warning and tried to find shelter. She even went past her old boyfriend's new place. "It was all dark and silent. But when I knocked, this thing came round the corner that wasn't even..." She giggles hysterically. "I ran. I climbed the gate in the car park, then I got the board out from beside the fire door."

Noah hunches. Madison sees that his jacket is torn at the shoulder, as if something had seized it with teeth.

"You both should have come to my place," says Madison. Then she remembers her mother's dead eyes and thinks *this is better*.

"Come on, let's go to Wardrobe," she tells Selene. "I'll fix your makeup."

"Thank you," she says, the tension draining out of her. "Just, thank you."

With clown white and black greasepaint, she manages to repair Selene's maquillage. There is an hour and half still to wait and, during that time, Ren texts them all the same message. He has an audition this afternoon. He will be late. Can they cover for him?

That they will do this is one of the unwritten rules of the House. They have all invoked it for one reason or another. Selene thinks it unwise to help him, in the circumstances, but Noah says he'll take over Lord Harrow's room and Madison replies with a "yes".

There is a knock at the door.

Giggles at her story. Squeals at the portrait. Thump and scream.

Shrieks at Selene. The snake. A missed beat. Madison finds herself holding her breath.

Noah's voice is not as loud as Ren's, and he laughs more, cackling as he yells, "I'll chop you into pizza! Yes, the idol demands pizza!" But the rhythm remains largely unchanged. Is it the rhythm? Madison wonders, averting her eyes from the abominations before her. Is it the rhythm that keeps them moving, that makes them obey the written rules?

Or is Ren right about their coming to see the freaks? Do they find us *funny*?

Ren arrives an hour in, and he is not in a good mood. "You know anything about someone breaking into the House?"

Noah looks to Madison, but Selene simply stares. Madison realizes she is checking Ren's eyes and his fingers.

"Supervisor caught me coming in. Had to pretend I was on a toilet break." Ren is wearing a black suit that *could* be Lord Harrow's costume. He frowns when he sees his hat in Noah's hands. "Anyway, they reckon a board had been pulled away from beside the fire door and someone had pissed out there. Asked if there was any damage inside. Did you even notice?"

"The board, yeah," says Noah. "We tried to put it back." He holds out the hat.

Ren snatches it up. "Were you going to tell anyone? If something's damaged, we'll all be held responsible!" He hasn't noticed the drape still lying across the lounge.

"Stop it! You're always on at him!" Selene steps up, corset jutting. "Well, I guess this means you're not a monster."

"Oh, not this again—"

"You're just a dick."

"Please, everybody!" Madison clutches her shawl. "Be quiet!"

There is a knock at the door. Without another word, Selene and Noah turn and march back up the hallway. Ren lingers a moment, breathing heavily as he bunches his curls back under the hat.

Madison asks, "What happened at the audition?"

He turns on her so suddenly she stumbles back into the chair. "I didn't get it, okay? I couldn't... I just *couldn't*, okay? I'm not what they want, so now I have to hang out here with a druggie and a loony and—" He breaks off, whirling into the wall of smoke. She hears his voice as he turns the corner and the trophy triggers. "I'll check the damage and take it all to Management this evening. You shouldn't have to worry."

Of course I do, she thinks. Now I have to worry about all of you.

Inside the House, it is always five minutes before midnight. Bells toll, the wind moans, and violins wail. Outside, the darkness comes intangibly, as Ren takes up his place and the monsters swarm.

Madison has no answer. Unless it was her accident that broke the world; in which case, what is the solution? She can't regrow her hand. By the end of shift, she has no better plan than the one she suggested before. "You come with me to my place," she tells Noah and Selene when they join her—they can hear Ren stomping and fussing with the board, searching for signs of unauthorized occupation. "We'll be safer together anyway."

She has re-hung the drape, kind of, but it won't pass more than a cursory inspection.

Sure enough, when the soundtrack dies and the overhead lights come on, Ren does not join them. He has gone out the fire door, avoiding them.

"He knows it was us," mutters Noah. "I say we ditch the costumes and get out *now*."

"We can ditch them in Wardrobe while he's talking to Management," says Madison. No point in making the trouble worse. "Selene, if you'll wait for us?"

Selene nods. Noah opens the door.

Electric rainbows still loop along the midway towards the entrance. The fairy-floss and slushie machines still resemble whole panes in a shattered cathedral. The Ferris wheel still turns, attempting to restock the sky as the Twirly Bird spins and spins. But they are not empty, as they should be at this hour. They are full.

Now, in Cinderella time, they have shed their footwear and eyeglasses, their teeth and rimes of hair. How pink it all is! How shiny! A stench arises from them like the ebb-tide of a poisoned sea. On the dodgems, their disgusting forms quiver and collapse into each other with every slam. In the boats of the Twirly Bird, some fling out extra arms to hold themselves in place as inertia sends ripples through whatever makes up their bodies.

"The moon!" gasps Selene. Madison does not look. She grabs Selene's hand and, after a fractional hesitation, offers her prosthetic to Noah. She cannot feel him take it, but there is weight, a comforting weight. "Across to the car park," she breathes. "Keep to the edge and don't look anyone in the eye." She takes a step, but the weight drags.

"It's no good," says Noah, his voice unnaturally calm. She looks and sees the shadows of the car park extrude things that look like hunting, like hunger. Where the light touches their skin, it is a slick and glistening pinky-gray. No ribs, no sockets, no sign of bone, just pure motion. Four legs touch the ground, but their faces are still human—as human as the rest, at least.

Madison can feel tears sliding down her cheeks. Her heart is pounding. "We have to get through," she whispers. "My mother—" And then she sees Ren.

Did he even get as far as Wardrobe? He stands by that unobtrusive door within a circle of gelid things, waving his arms and swaying as if he could fall at any moment. But even through her own fear, Madison sees this is not mindless panic. His arms move just fast enough to create an illusion of bonelessness. He puffs out his cheeks as he gyrates and bugs his eyes. The gelid creatures are pressing in, pressing together, but they leave him space. They watch him.

Out of the car park, one of the four-legs noses, slides into the light. Its jaw elongates, sagging, it spews a tongue. Does Ren see it? His gyrations grow wilder, he sinks lower, as if he is attempting to use his unwelcome audience as cover.

The hunting thing palpitates, focuses obscenely. Ignoring, or perhaps not seeing the little cluster at the front of the House, it slinks towards its prey.

Madison lets go of Selene's hand and reaches into her own right sleeve—the gray dress is roomy, she manages easily. The clips come undone. "Go back inside," she tells them. "I'm going to get him." Noah gasps as he realizes he is still holding her prosthetic.

She keeps to the edge, slipping and weaving. The four-legs can see her now, but nothing stops her before she reaches the food concession. The stall is untended, at least by anything she can recognize, but as staff herself, she is entitled to step in.

They notice my hand. Always.

Inside the fairy-floss machine, two wands spin sugar into pink and glistening clouds. She takes a deep breath, then reaches for the serving hatch. They were all taught to never ever put their hands into the machine, but she isn't inserting her hand. She inserts her stump.

She isn't trained, like Ren. She can't make her body twist, though she does her best. But what draws the creatures' attention, what makes them part for her as she approaches, is the sticky, pink globule of fairy floss woven around her right wrist. It looks almost like one of them. She waves it round, as if she is on the Twirly Bird. Before the four-legs can close the distance, the two-legs let her through to the crouching man. They watch her as they watch her in the House. There is a sequined shifting of eyes as she looms over him. Wonderingly, his own eyes turn upwards.

"Your shift isn't finished," she tells him, then offers the fairy-floss as if to help him up.

He meets her eyes. And then, without prelude, he bites into the sticky pink.

Her missing fingers prickle. The things ripple and chitter, they seem *pleased*. As Ren rises, they bubble and part, allowing him and her to retrace their steps.

On the threshold of the House, he pauses. "Oh Christ, it's nearly here!"

She does not look. Instead, she knocks: the special ratta-tat that means a cast member is outside. The door opens, and they slip in.

Noah is still holding her prosthetic. He waits until she has wiped the sticky remains from her stump, then presents it to her. Ren has collapsed on the lounge and is curling, curling up into a ball.

"What's happening?" he moans. "Why so many all of a sudden? Why here? Did they follow me?"

"Just couldn't admit it, could you?" Selene sits down beside him and, after a moment, pats his shoulder.

Her prosthetic reattached, Madison reaches behind the bear, to the switchboard. She turns the soundtrack back on. Swaps the overheads for the effects lighting.

"What are you doing?" Noah says. "We have to think of something—go out the fire door maybe and climb the fence."

"If we can hold out here till daylight," Ren sits up. "maybe we can make it to my car."

And go where? This is the world now. "Go to your rooms," she says. "It will be alright. Just keep up the rhythm."

There is a knock at the door.

Itch in the Party House

Ivy Grimes

SHELLEY DIDN'T WANT Agnes to die. She just wanted to kill her.

After the first killing, everything had texture. Walking into the night felt like rubbing a velvet hem across her face. The streetlights' glow pricked her skin. The lingering odor of baked bread from a neighboring apartment made her feel like she was breathing in a cumulous cloud. She puffed up.

It was almost dawn when she fell asleep, satisfied. The feeling was gone when she woke up that afternoon. That was when the thought recurred, came back to whir and whir. Kill Agnes again. Kill Agnes again.

Shelley had only been a real estate agent for nine months, and her boss had subjected her to his traditional initiation for new agents by giving her the Party House that never sold. The agency had tried to sell it for the previous two decades and seemed to keep it around as kind of a joke. The boss said the owner was an old friend of his, stuck with the house as his inheritance. Since the owner was rich, he didn't mind the taxes and upkeep expenses, but he refused to have the place remodeled. The house had belonged to his parents, and he must have been sentimental about it. The

Party House was billed as a fixer-upper, shown to buyers who wanted something with character and quirky charm.

As long as people were early in their house search, they enjoyed the tour. They marveled at the centerpiece, an indoor pool in the living room. The pool had four little streams leading to the four main bedrooms.

A dry hallway ran around the house, and Shelley took her guests that longer way so they could see the bedrooms, which made some people laugh and others titter. The rooms had ceiling mirrors and neon shag carpets and glittery chandeliers and heart-shaped beds. Each room was a little different (one decorated in leopard print, another in tie-dye), yet the point of each was the same. The bedrooms were the logical conclusion to the living room pool.

The whole house smelled like sour milk. At night, Shelley imagined halos of flame circling each doorway. Why did she start going at night? If only she had never. But one night, she realized she had forgotten to lock up after a showing, so she had to go back. After that, it was irresistible.

Agnes lived in a fifth bedroom that didn't fit the theme of the Party House. Her door was kept shut, and Shelley's boss had told her the room was a supply closet. It was a lie. The room wasn't spacious, but it fit a twin bed and a nightstand with a small lamp.

That first time Shelley opened the room, she tried unsuccessfully to find a light switch. She had her flashlight, and she pointed it around the room to see what the sexy theme was. But no, it was a simple Victorian sort of room. For people with a *Jane Eyre* kink?

There was a lump in the bed, and it moved. Someone sat up, pushed away tousled hair, and turned on the lamp to reveal the face of an elderly woman.

Shocked, Shelley backed away. She'd heard of people camping out in houses for sale, but she hadn't come up with a plan for how to deal with it. What if the woman had a gun under her pillow? Anything was possible, so Shelley opted to be very gentle with the woman.

"Who are you?" the woman said with the wavery voice of an octogenarian.

"Shelley, the real estate agent. I'm not going to hurt you. I'll just leave now."

"The real estate agent? It's about time they sold this place. You go on about your business and don't mind me."

Shelley stared. The woman rubbed her eyes, which were coated with a milky film. Something twisted inside Shelley's body—and suddenly she knew. The woman was a ghost.

"I'm Agnes," the woman said with an innocent smile.

"You're haunting this place," Shelley said, hoping that like a hero in a fairy tale, she would be rewarded for being forthright.

"What are you talking about, dear? I'm Sadie's grandmother. The owner lets me live here while I'm recuperating. But it's much too loud here for me. Parties, day and night."

Then Agnes stopped moving, stopped talking. She stared at Shelley unblinking, her milky eyes wide, her face a mask of fear.

"What? What?" Shelley asked as the woman stared back at her with the contempt of an angel holding a scythe, a scythe to turn the unworthy into ribbons of anonymous flesh and bone.

Shelley wasn't unworthy, though. She wasn't evil. Seconds of silence passed before she gained the courage to move again. She began to back away, stumbling over her feet on her way out.

Her movement seemed to wake the woman. Agnes's eyes widened even more, and she began to scream. Like an alarm. As if someone was dying.

Shelley kept scuttling backwards, slowing her own progress, afraid to turn her back lest the woman—what? Jump on her back and bite her neck when she wasn't looking?

She finally got outside, leaving the front door unlocked again, no time to stop. She dropped her keys twice before managing to open her car door, and she turned the ignition with trembling hands.

The Party House was off by itself (with no neighbors to complain about the noise and debauchery), off in the middle of the woods. She would have screamed, but she knew there would be no one to hear her. In her panic, her fingers couldn't seem to feel what she was doing, but somehow she backed out of the driveway and sped away.

Sweating. Furious. Embarrassed. Had she imagined the old woman? Already, she felt a tickle in her heart, a tickle in her fingers. There was a craving deep inside her. "Go back," the voice whispered. "Go back."

As a child, Shelley had been possessed by a few fixations. When the family dog died, she forced herself to kiss it on the head seven times before her mother took it to the vet to be obliterated. When she found a dead bird smushed to the sidewalk outside her house, she had made herself take a stick to the corpse, to poke and lift it to see different angles, even though it was the last thing she wanted to do.

There were good things, too—she had to brush her teeth seven times a day, and pray seven times, and say her multiplications tables seven times. She had it all spaced out. She even used an alarm clock to alert her when it was time to perform a ritual. Not that she needed it. The voice inside her was so loud, it could wake her from a sound sleep. That was the voice she heard again, and now it was talking to her about Agnes.

She called her boss and left a message that night to tell him there was a woman living at the house. Then she got into bed and turned off the lights. That scream kept invading her dreams, though, calling like a siren from a police car circling the neighborhood. An alarm. An alarm. Something had gone wrong. If only she hadn't gone to the house at night and looked so thoroughly.

The next morning, she woke up to a message from her boss that said: "What were you smoking last night, Shell? The house is just a joke. Just show it to people who need a laugh. Then we'll give it to the next new hire. Or prove me wrong and sell it yourself!"

So simple to him. But he didn't say if there was a woman named Agnes who lived in the house. Or who had died in the house. He didn't respond to those claims at all. She wanted to call him immediately and grill him, but she didn't want to risk seeming like she'd lost it. She needed the job, after all, and leaving so quickly and for no good reason wouldn't look good on her resume. It wouldn't look good at all.

There were two options—keep away from the house or return to it. Keeping away was the right choice. But the voice inside said to return.

"Look again. Look again." That's what it said. Just like with the dead dog and the dead bird. Shelley had to see that awful face again. She had to see Agnes again.

That day was ordinary, full of client meetings and paperwork, but that night, she finally obeyed the voice. If she ignored the voice, it would get louder and louder, and she knew she would give in eventually. The only other option was to live with a permanent itch in the brain, a nag a nag a nag that never went away.

The door to Agnes's room had been shut overnight. Had Agnes shut it?

"Open it," the voice said. "See what's inside."

Darkness again. Her flashlight found the lump in the bed, and Agnes sat up, revealing her ancient face.

"It's Shelley."

Agnes gave her a wide wide smile with her eyes of frosted glass.

"I wanted to see if you were really here."

"I am. I always am."

"Why are you still here? You must be dead, I mean. A ghost."

Agnes laughed. "People think the strangest things about me. But I'm the only good person around here, and scum people always hate good people."

Didn't Agnes know she was a ghost?

"Why are you staring at me?" Agnes said, her voice quavering more than usual. She opened her mouth, but it froze in place; the shape of it fascinated Shelley. It was poised in some eternal rhombus. Agnes had frozen again, like she had the night before.

This was bad. Bad. That frozen face awakened a deep terror (and equivalent pleasure) in Shelley. It was time. Agnes had to be killed. Agnes wanted to be killed. Shelley wanted Agnes to be killed. The universe wanted it. It was time.

"Kill her," Shelley whispered to herself. "Kill her."

Another, quieter voice inside Shelley asked why it was necessary to kill Agnes. Wasn't she already dead? Maybe. Maybe not. That wasn't the point. The point was that she had to be *killed*.

Shelley picked up her heavy flashlight, held it high over her head, and shone it on Agnes like Agnes was a suspect trying to escape. A twinkle in that old eye told Shelley that Agnes knew what was happening. It was an old ritual.

Then the scream came, the kind of sound that could pull sinew from sinew, bone from bone.

And Shelley brought the flashlight down on the old woman's head, down down down with the weight of the ocean. The head crumpled like aluminum foil—no skull. No blood. It felt so good to see. It wasn't like a dead dog or a dead bird. It was righteous vengeance. Something had been killed that needed to be killed. The universe was working through Shelley's hands.

She slept well that night, and the next day she showed off the Party House to a quirky young couple who said they wanted to live somewhere truly strange. They laughed when they saw the house, and naturally, they didn't really want it. Shelley opened all the doors to all the bedrooms except the one where Agnes slept. She didn't want them to see the murder scene. When the couple was occupied, going through the other bedrooms and laughing and admiring, Shelley took a quick peek in the forbidden bedroom. The room was plunged in night even in daylight since it had no windows. Shelley used her cell phone light to shine on the places where she had left the corpse of Agnes, and she truly wasn't sure what she would find. A dead body? An angry ghost? A screaming old woman?

There was a lump in the bed. On the floor was the severed, crumpled head of Agnes. Crumpled like a piece of tinfoil. She moved closer to the bed and pulled back the blankets, and she found Agnes fully formed again, her head intact. She was sleeping so peacefully, her chest slowly rising and falling.

Agnes opened one eye and said, "Not yet. It's still daytime."

"What's in here?"

Shelley heard a voice full of amusement calling to her from outside the room. The couple. She had almost forgotten her job.

"Oh, nothing!" Shelley laughed as she turned off her phone's light and emerged from the room. "Just a broom closet. No light switch."

The couple was disappointed that they'd seen it all, but they were ready to move on and find their perfect house. A quirky house, yes, but not that quirky.

Kill Agnes again. Kill Agnes again. The voice came to her every night, just after the sunset. She killed Agnes night after night, until over a dozen crumpled heads lay on the floor. The heads were piled up like balls of paper from some artist who was sketching, tossing out idea after idea.

Each night after she did her deed, Shelley felt the texture of the world. New textures came every night. Listening to music was like pulling a string of colorful handkerchiefs from her ear. Lighting a candle in her bedroom and holding out her hands to be warmed by the tiny flame, she felt like she was touching the pulsing body of a tiny animal.

"Why, though?" she kept asking herself. "Why do I have to kill Agnes? Why?"

After two weeks of killing Agnes, she woke up in the middle of the night and found the textures already fading. The voice was already begging her, already preparing for the next night when she would need to kill Agnes again.

"But what am I becoming?" Shelley said. "If I need to kill every night?"

She began to cry, thinking of all those heads, those crumpled heads. It was as if God had finally made someone he couldn't love and then kept on making them.

"I'm not a monster," Shelley said.

She called her boss, planning to leave a message saying she couldn't stand the house anymore, that it couldn't be sold, and that she was giving up her key. Sometimes in a flash people can change like that—if they give away the key. But the temptation is so great to make a copy of the key before returning it. That's what Shelley would have done if her boss hadn't answered, if Shelley had simply left a message and gone to sleep and woken up the next day.

Her boss answered, though. "Why are you calling in the middle of the night? You woke up my girlfriend! It better be an emergency."

"It is!" Shelly couldn't stop her tears, couldn't stay professional. "That house is haunted. Why did you give it to me? Why?"

Silence. Her boss breathed into the phone.

"Ghosts aren't real. The police will never believe you."

"It's haunted," Shelley insisted.

"Well. My friend who owns the house…that's me. It was my parents' house. I was just a little kid when I lived there."

Shelley began to breathe hard. She covered the phone so he wouldn't hear her. She was working for a monster. It was all his fault.

"You might have met a ghost or two in the house. I mean, I believe you. Most people won't. I remember the good times there—the laughter and the swimming and the smell of maraschino cherries. Anytime I wanted, I could jump in the pool! Even in my pajamas. Can you imagine?"

She nodded. The smells from past parties lingered in the air. Even in Agnes's room.

"There were some bad things that happened, allegedly. But I was just a kid."

"Who killed Agnes?" Shelley said. How dare he reminisce while Agnes was killed over and over and over again?

"Agnes was a friend of the family," her boss said. "I loved her. But she was mean. So, everyone hated her. Even me. Have you ever loved someone and hated them at the same time?"

"You killed her," Shelley whispered, knowing she had said a thing that shouldn't be said.

"I didn't say that!" her boss said, screaming into the phone. "Anyone could have done it. Are your hands clean?"

"It could have been anyone who killed her," Shelley said, looking down at her hands that had crumpled so many heads.

"She didn't belong in the Party House. She was a threat...you see what she's done to it. You don't know how special that house was. Is. And you know what?" His voice got quiet. "She wants you to do it."

"So, when someone kills her, you're saying...it's a relief?"

"It's a good thing for everyone, Shelley."

If that was true, then she had done many good deeds. But she couldn't anymore. She was afraid it was changing her in fundamental, microscopic ways.

"I don't want the house," Shelley said, trying to sound professional, to swallow her anger. "You've burdened me so you could have your peace—so you wouldn't have to face her. So you could get rid of the responsibility."

"But if we ever sell the place, what will happen to her? Maybe something even worse. If you've really had enough, I'll take it back."

"I've really had enough."

"You didn't last as long as the rest. But you're softer. I get it. It's too bad, because you had so much promise. I can tell you're someone with a strong spirit deep inside. But we'll forget it, and you can keep your job as long as you keep selling ordinary houses."

All her coworkers! All the people hired by her boss—they'd all been murderers. Night after night until they couldn't take it anymore.

He continued. "And there were rewards, weren't there? It was...beautiful, wasn't it?" her boss said, a perverse note creeping into his voice.

"I don't know," Shelley said, which made him laugh. It was too mixed-up to say that he was right. To give him that.

He agreed to take back the key the next morning and hire a new employee. A new keeper of the key.

She considered getting back into bed, following the plan. But all those crumpled pages, discarded scribblings of God—she couldn't stand it. Whatever had happened before, back then, it had to end. She grabbed what she needed, and she got back in her car and drove back to the Party House. It was still quite dark when she arrived.

She used her key and went inside, to the room that had called to her so many times. Agnes's head hadn't grown back yet. That wouldn't happen until morning. The bloodless stump of her neck poked from the covers.

Shelley put a box of matches beside the bed.

"If you want it to end, then end it!" she shouted to the crumpled heads. To the headless lump in the bed.

The next morning when Shelley gave the key back to her boss, she smiled. All day, she waited for news that the house had burned down.

But it didn't happen. A new employee was hired, and things went on.

After a week of waiting for the house to burn, Shelley couldn't take it anymore. Agnes was too determined to be killed or too confused about how to end it all. Shelley had relinquished her grip on the house when she turned in the key, but she still drove by sometimes at night and looked up at the empty, lightless house, imagining the parties that once were.

So, she moved away—three hours away. Another agency hired her, and her boss didn't even ask why she'd left her last job.

The insistent voice (which had always been with her) still prodded her sometimes. It was even louder now than it had been when she was a child. Agnes must have done that to her. "Watch something awful," it would say to her sometimes, or "Put one finger in the fire to see if it burns."

If she resisted the voice, she would have bad dreams. She would dream she was swimming in the Party House, swimming from bedroom to bedroom, seeing sights no child should see, all while looking for Agnes. If she did the little tasks the voice required, she would dream of nothing. Blessed nothing. It was the best thing she could hope for.

CONTRIBUTORS

Jason Barnett is a self-taught, freelance artist and designer from Dallas, Texas, currently living and working in Portland, Oregon.

Julie Blankenship is an artist whose mixed media work includes painting on 19th-century photographs with ink, dust and glue. Exploring beauty, and the fragile nature of identity, her work alludes to metamorphoses, dark histories and gothic struggles. Publications include *Blood Bath, Poets & Writers Magazine, London Reader, Sein und Werden,* and *Of One Pure Will,* Egaeus Press (cover). Exhibitions include projects at Amsterdam Center for Photography, Amsterdam; American Institute of Architects, and Walter/McBean Gallery, San Francisco; group shows at CICA Museum, Seoul; Center for Photography International, Haarlem; *Silent Fire* collaboration by Yale Institute of Sacred Music + Nasty Women Connecticut; *Nordic Folktales Revisited,* Nordic Northwest, Portland; and (upcoming) *Museum of No Spectators,* Burning Man. She lives in San Francisco. Instagram @privateyesf.

Daniel Braum is the author of the short story collections *The Night Marchers and Other Strange Tales* (Cemetery Dance), *The Wish Mechanics: Stories of the Strange and Fantastic* (Independent Legions) and the Dim Shores Press chapbook, *Yeti Tiger Dragon*. His third collection, *Underworld Dreams,* is from Lethe Press. His first novella, *The Serpent's Shadow,* is out now from Cemetery Dance eBooks and is coming soon in a print edition. He is the editor of the *Spirits Unwrapped* anthology and the host and founder of the Night Time Logic reading series and the annual New York Ghost Story Festival. His work is forthcoming in several anthologies and has appeared in the *The Best Horror of the Year Volume 12* edited by Ellen Datlow. His novel *Servant of the Eighth Wind* is forthcoming from Lethe Press. He can be found at bloodandstardust.wordpress.com, www.facebook.com/DanielBraumFiction, and on twitter @danielbraum.

Chris Brawley (Ph.D.) is a professor of Humanities at Central Piedmont in Charlotte, North Carolina. He has published papers on C.S. Lewis, J.R.R. Tolkien, George MacDonald, and Thomas Ligotti. His book *Nature and the Numinous in Mythopoeic Fantasy* was published by MacFarland in 2014.

Kristin Cleaveland writes horror and dark fiction. Her work has been published in *Southwest Review*, *Excuse Me Magazine*, *Black Telephone Magazine*, and more. Her poem "Siren Song" recently appeared in *Musings of the Muses*, and her short fiction has been included in the anthologies *Blood & Bone: An Anthology of Body Horror by Women and Non-Binary Writers* and *Ravens & Roses: A Women's Gothic Anthology*, among others. She is an affiliate member of the Horror Writers Association. Find her on Twitter as @KristinCleaves.

Armel Dagorn is now back in his native France after living in Ireland for seven years. His writing has appeared in such places as *Weird Horror, Lamplight, Nightscript* and *The Shadow Booth*, as well as in the anthologies *Haunted Futures* and *Strange California*. His short story collection *The Proverb Zoo* was published in 2018 by The Dreadful Press.

Lucy Frost is an Arabic-American transgender woman poet from Austin, Texas. Her work includes "Discourse on Supernatural Horror," a long poem dedicated to Thomas Ligotti; parts of it are forthcoming in an anthology by Gutslut Press. Lucy's work has also appeared in *Wrongdoing Magazine, Perhappened Magazine*, and elsewhere. She can be found on Twitter @intomymachine.

Ivy Grimes lives in Virginia. Her writing has appeared in *Vastarien, Dark Matter Magazine, Potomac Review, Daily Science Fiction*, and elsewhere. On Twitter, she is @IvyGri.

Macy Harrison is a horror and dark fantasy writer and literature teacher based in Dallas, Texas. Her fiction has most recently appeared in the anthologies *Deadsteam II* and *The Witches Ball*.

Vivian Kasley hails from the land of the strange and unusual, Florida! She's a writer of short stories and poetry that have appeared in various science fiction anthologies, horror anthologies, horror magazines, and webzines. Some of her street cred includes Grimscribe Press, Ghost Orchid Press, *Diabolica Americana*, The Denver Horror Collective's *Jewish Book of Horror*, Kandisha Press's *Slash-Her*, and poetry in Black Spot Books inaugural women in horror poetry showcase, *Under Her Skin*. When not writing or subbing at the local middle school, she spends her time reading in bubble baths, snuggling her rescue cats and dogs, going on foodie adventures with her other half, and searching for seashells and other treasures along the beach.

Gwendolyn Kiste is the three-time Bram Stoker Award-winning author of *The Rust Maidens, Reluctant Immortals, Boneset & Feathers, And Her Smile Will Untether the Universe, Pretty Marys All in a Row*, and *The Invention of Ghosts*. Her short fiction and nonfiction have appeared in *Nightmare Magazine, Best American Science Fiction and Fantasy, Vastarien*, Tor's *Nightfire, Black Static, The Dark, Daily Science Fiction, Interzone*, and *LampLight*, among others. Originally from Ohio, she now resides on an abandoned horse farm outside of Pittsburgh with her husband, two cats, and not nearly enough ghosts. Find her online at gwendolynkiste.com.

Joe Koch (he/they) writes literary horror and surrealist trash. Joe is a Shirley Jackson Award finalist and the author of *The Wingspan of Severed Hands, The Couvade*, and *Convulsive*. They've had over fifty short stories published in books and journals like *Year's Best Hardcore Horror, The Queer Book of Saints*, and *Not All Monsters*. Find Joe online at horrorsong.blog and on Twitter @horrorsong.

Romana Lockwood is a lady, and ladies do not reveal their age. Her many incarnations have included nurse in a devastating war, typist, war correspondent, television news anchor, housewife, waitress, and columnist. Her column "In My Eyes," which ran from 19__ to 20__ was, in the eyes of many, a serious contender for the Pulitzer Prize, or at the very least the Horace Greeley or the Breindel awards. Her first marriage was to Ernest James Hayden, a shoe salesman, who passed in 19__ from a failure of the heart, the variety that physicians refer to as "massive." Of her second marriage she does not speak. She rejects in toto the Abrahamic religions. She takes daily walks, her coffee black, her cats calico, and her tea sweet.

Erik McHatton's passion for horror literature began in grade school and can be credited to an early fascination with the "Terrific Triples" horror collections of Helen Hoke. He began writing fiction seriously in 2019 and has since been published several times in print and online publications. He hopes to follow in the footsteps of authors like Ligotti, CAS, Bloch, Jackson, Barker, and Cushing. He lives in Kentucky with his beautiful wife and kids, along with dear friends and family.

Lindz McLeod is a queer, working-class, Scottish writer who dabbles in the surreal. Her prose has been published by *Catapult, Flash Fiction Online, Pseudopod*, and many more. She is a full member of the SFWA and is represented by Headwater Literary Management.

T.M. Morgan has been published in *Vastarien, Lamplight, Penumbric*, and *Mythaxis*, and in the anthology *Tales From Omnipark*. He has upcoming work in *Pseudopod, Sley House, The Wicked Library*, an *Apokrapha* (*Lamplight*) radio play, and in the anthology *Vinyl Cuts*. He is the editor of DreadImaginings.com. You can read more about him at thetmmorgan.wordpress.com.

Logan Noble is an award-winning horror writer who spends his days with his wife and pets. His short stories have appeared in a number of anthologies and magazines, including *Pickman's Gallery, Miskatonic Dreams, Déraciné Magazine*, and *Sanitarium Magazine*. His complete works can be found at logannobleauthor.com.

Vishnu Shyamala Prasad is from Kerala, India, currently living and working in the United Arab Emirates. He has been drawing since as far back as he can remember.

Erica Ruppert, HWA, lives in northern New Jersey with her husband and too many cats. She writes weird horror and dark fantasy, and her work has appeared in magazines including *Unnerving, Lamplight*, and *Nightmare*, on podcasts including *PodCastle*, and in multiple anthologies. When she is not writing, she runs, bakes, and gardens with more enthusiasm than skill. Her novella, *Sisters in Arms*, was released by Trepidatio Publishing in July 2021.

Contributors

Æ Trueman is a long time visual artist and the cover designer for *Vastarien*. She lives in the wilds of New Jersey.

Wendy N. Wagner is the editor-in-chief of *Nightmare Magazine* and the managing/senior editor of *Lightspeed*. Her short stories, essays, and poems run the gamut from horror to environmental literature. Her longer work includes the novella *The Secret Skin*, the horror novel *The Deer Kings*, the Locus bestselling SF eco-thriller *An Oath of Dogs*, and two novels for the Pathfinder role-playing game. She lives in Oregon with her very understanding family, two large cats, and a Muppet disguised as a dog. You can find her at winniewoohoo.com.

Kyla Lee Ward's credits include the Stoker-nominated "And In Her Eyes The City Drowned," the collection *The Macabre Modern and Other Morbidities*, and tales in *Gods, Memes and Monsters: A Twenty-first Century Bestiary* and *Hear Me Roar: Tales of Real Women and Unreal Worlds*. Going back a little further, my novel *Prismatic* (co-authored as Edwina Grey) won an Aurealis Award for best horror novel.

Alvaro Zinos-Amaro is a Hugo and Locus finalist with some forty stories published in numerous magazines and anthologies, including *Lackington's, The Journal of Unlikely Entomology, Analog, Lightspeed, Beneath Ceaseless Skies, Galaxy's Edge, Nature*, and volumes such as *The Year's Best Science Fiction & Fantasy, The Mammoth Book of Jack the Ripper Stories, This Way to the End Times, Shades Within Us: Tales of Migrations* and *Fractured Borders, Blood Business, The Unquiet Dreamer: A Tribute to Harlan Ellison*, the recent *Nox Pareidolia*, and the forthcoming *It Came from the Multiplex*.

www.ingramcontent.com/pod-product-compliance
Lightning Source LLC
LaVergne TN
LVHW021951060526
838201LV00049B/1667